LEAN MANAGEMENT

TOOLS AND TECHNIQUES

SATHEESH RAJU G

Contents

Preface *v*

Acknowledgements *vii*

1. Lean Management 1

2. Lean Tools And Techniques 21

3. Lean System 44

4. Project Selection For Lean 82

5. Lean Management And Implementation 102

Abrevations 129

Preface

Lean management and lean practices have given firms an opportunity to make big chances in improving the productivity. Indian firms have taken advantage by implementing lean practices but majority of the small and medium are yet to understand lean processes. Efficiency has become important for both manufacturing and service industry. Manufacturing cost is a crucial element in this competitive global environment. Indian firms need to understand the lean concepts and the methods to implement them.

Implementation of lean practices are going to play vital role in transforming small and micro industries into large scale industries. There is a need for better understanding of lean practices by Indian firms to gain competitive advantage internationally. Minimizing the non-value creation activities and eliminating them continuous improvement is going to be a step for success for Indian firms in global market.

This book emphasizes on giving basic information about lean practices and tools and techniques which can be easily understood by small and micro entrepreneurs. Indian manufacturers are very much aware of minimizing the waste but its time to become much more familiar with proven lean techniques. It has focused more on established practices and written in common language where a common lay man can understand and implement lean practices.

Acknowledgements

Manny of my collegues and students were very helpfull in coming out with this book. I express my special appreciation to my colleagues Dr.N.Suman Kumar and D.Ramesh Babu for their valuable inputs. I specially thank Dr.L.Sampath for his valuable support in bringing this book out.

CHAPTER I

Lean Management

Lean Management

- Introduction
- Evolution of lean
- Need for lean management
- Elements of lean management
- Lean manufacturing and global competition
- Seven wastes
- Value flow analysis
- Muda, Muri, and Mura
- Meeting the stake holders' requirements

Today's businesses need to be managed effectively without wasting the resources such as time, effort, and money. Customer satisfaction needs improvement at a rate where it turns as a competitive advantage for the businesses. Improving the product standards and service quality standards has become mandatory. The effective way of fulfilling all the above is implementing the lean practices. Lean management has become popular and there is a need to understand it.

Introduction

Lean management is a continuous process of improvement in manufacturing. It is a methodology that is designed to improve the efficiency and quality by eliminating the wastes. To achieve efficiency and quality there is a need for changes in the process of manufacturing either in small or incremental. Lean management is directed towards producing best and valuable products and services for the customers. Beside producing value for its customers lean management also focuses on optimizing the resources, it eliminates the steps which results in waste of time, effort, and money. Lean management is also called as lean manufacturing and lean production. The idea of lean management is to produce only the best and most valuable services and products to the customers at the right place. In brief, lean manufacturing seeks to implement business processes that achieve high quality, safety and worker morale, whilst reducing cost and shortening lead times. This in itself is not unique to Japan. What sets lean management apart, and makes it particularly effective, is that it has at its core a laser-sharp focus on the elimination of all waste from all processes.

Toyota initially practiced and introduced it to the world but it has become a widely adopted practice among British and European startups. It is been implemented in diversified industries both in manufacturing and software development. The startups starte3d to develop framework to their businesses which focus on delivering value to the customers by eliminating waste and continuously improving processes.

History of Lean management

Henry Ford was one of the first people to develop the ideas behind Lean Manufacturing. He used the idea of "continuous flow" on the assembly line for his Model T automobile, where he kept production standards extremely tight, so each stage of the process fitted together with each other stage, perfectly. This resulted in little waste.

But Ford's process wasn't flexible. His assembly lines produced the same thing, again and again, and the process didn't easily allow for any modifications or changes to the product – a Model T assembly line produced only the Model T. It was also a "push" process, where Ford set the level of production, instead of a "pull" process led by consumer demand. This led to large inventories of unsold automobiles, ultimately resulting in lots of wasted money.

Other manufacturers began to use Ford's ideas, but many realized that the inflexibility of his system was a problem. Taiichi Ohno of Toyota then developed the Toyota Production System (TPS), which used Just In Time manufacturing methods to increase efficiency. As Womack reported in his book, Toyota used this process successfully and, as a result, eventually emerged as one the most profitable manufacturing companies in the world.

Toyota based lean manufacturing is based on two basic concepts.

The first, known as Jidoka, states that quality must be an inherent part of the overall process. Reviewing items at the end of the production line isn't the most efficient way to deliver quality products to consumers. The second component called Just-in-Time, which is a supply and demand idea that states materials and products should be made only when needed. Just-in-Time reduces cost and waste associated with inventory backlogs.

The history of lean management or lean manufacturing is traced back to the early years of Toyota and the development of the Toyota Production System after Japan's defeat in WWII when the company was looking for a means to compete with the US car industry through developing and implementing a range of low-cost improvements within their business. The concept of lean management originated in the Japanese manufacturing industry in the 1990s, beginning with the Toyota Production System (TPS). Because Toyota was initially a small automobile manufacturer that eventually became successful on a global scale, it's business, and operational process quickly caught on. Other companies soon began to adopt similar methodologies with the hope of achieving the same level of success. Today, lean management is widely used by leading businesses around the world, including Intel, John Deere, and Nike.

Principles of Lean Management

Lean management revolves around these core principles: defining value, mapping stream value, creating flow, establishing pull, and pursuing perfection.

- **Defining Value**

Value is defined by the customer needs for a specific product. This principle identifies the value of a product or service from the customer's perspective. For example, what is the time line for manufacturing and delivering, what is the price at which the product is offered to the customer, what are the other important requirements and expectations that must be met, this information helps in defining the value.

- **Mapping Stream Value**

Once defining value is finished the next step is mapping value stream. This principle is also known as waste mapping. It examines all steps from raw materials to delivering the final product to the customer. Value stream mapping acts as a eye opener in identifying all steps that take place in producing a product or service through a process. The process can be in design, procurement, production, human resources, administration, sales, delivery and customer service. Putting this process map on one page which includes flow of material to product conversion and delivery to the customer will helps to identify the steps that does not create value and find ways to eliminate those wasteful steps. Value stream mapping can be referred as process re-engineering and helps in understanding the entire business process.

- **Creating Flow**

Once the value streaming is mapped the next step is to create the flow. This principle focuses on attaining efficiency and speed, as well as ensuring that multiple operational tasks are completed as quickly and smoothly as possible without sacrificing quality. Value creation steps should occur in tight sequence so that the product or service will flow smoothly toward the customer.

- **Establishing Pull**

With improved flow time to market can dramatically improve. Create a flow in which there are just enough materials and resources to create the required products on time and in a continuous fashion. This makes to manufacture and deliver products as needed as just in time. This makes the customer buy the product when he requires it often in weeks instead of months. As a result products don't need to be built in advance or materials stock pilled, creating expensive inventory that needs to be managed.

- **Pursuing Perfection**

The most important step is to make lean thinking and process improvement as part of our organizational culture. Really, this means making sure that the other four principles occur continuously and consistently. Make sure all employees are also on board with the ultimate lean mission. Lean is not a static system it requires constant effort and vigilance to perfect.

Benefits of Lean Management

Companies that apply lean management methodologies typically have one goal in mind: continuous improvement. By implementing these lean principles, they often reach this goal by saving time and therefore money. They also can improve customer satisfaction rates, which can lead to increased revenue from referrals and repeat business.

Further, becoming proficient in lean management can be an invaluable investment. Our Lean Management Certification Training program teaches students crucial lean management skills that won't just help them in their current role, but will also help them to be successful in other opportunities they may pursue in the future.

In this training program, students learn about all aspects of lean management, and how these principles can be applied in services, manufacturing, and general business roles. Students learn about the various tools in lean management, common types of waste, and ways to eliminate it to improve overall business efficiency. Students enrolled in this course receive five hours of e-learning content, a downloadable e-book, and other resources that are useful for all skill levels. Once completed, students earn a lean management certification.

Elements of lean Manufacturing

The goal of lean manufacturing is to minimize the amount of time and resources used in manufacturing and other activities of business with emphasis on eliminating all forms of wastage.

Kaizen

Kaizen, a Japanese term for "change" or "improvement," serves as a sort of blueprint for lean production. It's based on the philosophy that production improvements should be continual and line-worker involvement is critical because they have the best view of the situation. The goal is to reduce waste and improve process flow. Each step of current production is documented, with such factors as production time and distance travelled, scrap rate, changeovers, bottlenecks, and product quality carefully measured. When process flow changes are made, new metrics are developed so that gains can be proven and quantified. At an automotive line, that might entail a closer physical proximity between wheel and axle assembly workstations to decrease production time.

5S Workplace Organization

The driving philosophy behind 5S workplace organization is that inefficient workplaces can't yield efficient production. Plant management must take the following five steps to organize physical surroundings before real change can be made: sort, set in order, shine, standardize, and sustain. Sorting involves designing stations for smooth and efficient workflow. Each tool is scrutinized for its value to the job, and irrelevant items are removed. The concept of setting in order involves organizing critical tools and equipment for proper storage and easy accessibility. Shining refers to plant cleanliness. In addition to creating a more appealing work environment, this makes it easier to see machine leaks and other failures. Standardizing is a way of formalizing practices and assigning responsibilities that will maintain the effect of the first three "S" strategies. Sustaining is the ability to maintain and continually enhance these efficiency practices. What are the minimum number of steps and processes needed in the car plant example? Anything more would be discontinued for inefficiency.

Cellular Manufacturing

Cellular manufacturing, also known as "continuous product flow," recognizes that for maximum efficiency, each stage of production must work in smooth unison with adjoining stages. With that in mind, manufacturers configure their plant so that production can flow quickly and easily from one workstation, or "cell," to the next. Machinery and equipment are regularly maintained to avoid downtime, and the plant is designed for the efficient staging of inventory. Raw materials in the car plant example are positioned where needed for the most strategic workflow.

Just-in-Time Production

The strategy of just-in-time production was developed by the Japanese automaker Toyota in the 1970s as a way of shaving inventory costs. In addition to the actual cost of buying and holding raw materials that can't immediately be used and sold, manufacturers must also assume the labor costs of handling and storing inventory and the physical cost of warehousing that material. The philosophy behind just-in-time production is to buy and store only the bare minimum number of materials needed for each stage of production. This requires a close relationship between cells so that the workflows from stage to stage without bottlenecks from a shortage of materials. In other words, carburettors are expensive and unwieldy to warehouse, so the auto plant example will take daily delivery and turn over inventory in 24 hours.

Lean manufacturing and global competition

Insightful implementation of lean is necessary for high value manufacturing and is complementary to strategic decision making to gain competitive advantage. Lean is difficult to implement as it has many tools to apply and should be aware when to apply these tools. Change management will be a factor in adopting lean practices as lean implementation is a transformational process. The implementation of lean practices should help in organizational development by improving the process. Organizations should prioritize in implementation of lean methods that helps in organizational development.

Lean implementation involves transformation of organizations. Lean focuses on reduction of cycle time, a cycle time is the length of time taken to convert raw materials into finished goods. The company which reduces cycle time when compared to its competitors will be able to respond more quickly to market demands and thus gain a large market share. Some of the benefits organization gets by reducing the cycle time are

- Innovation opportunities: The organizations will have time to focus on innovations
- Better distribution positioning: It gives an opportunity for the organization to distribute just in time which leads to better distribution positioning.
- Increased productivity: by shortening cycle time and increasing more man hours it increases the productivity.
- Higher customer satisfaction: Lean helps in identifying the value as defined by the customer which helps in satisfying more customers.

The organization can determine better ways of converting assets quickly into profits. It also helps in meeting competitive demands of evolving markets, the focus on single component will eliminate the waste and inefficiency. This will result in quality and helps in acting towards customer driven solution. Lean manufacturing powerfully enables the manufacturers to navigate with changing market conditions with precision and streamline and simplify the production process to gain competitive advantage.

Seven wastes

Eliminating waste is one of the major prerequisites for building a successful company. wasteful activities need to be identified and should be eliminated; this concept is an integral part of lean thinking. Lean manufacturing is primarily derived from the Toyato production system aims at integrating each step of production into a holistic, efficient process that reduces cost and improves overall revenue. Taichi Ohno who is considered as one of the founding fathers of lean manufacturing has established a solid efficient work process

Lean manufacturing identifies seven wastes in manufacturing, optimizing the process to eliminate waste is crucial. The lean theory describes 7 major areas

1.

Over production

Over production is the most obvious form of manufacturing waste. It not only leads to depleted raw materials but also to wasted storage and excess capital tied up in unused products. Stocking too many leads to obvious costs like storage, wasted materials and excessive capital tied up in unused or useless inventory. Producing more means exceeding customers demand which leads to additional costs. Over production leads to other six types of wastes. The reason is that excess products or tasks require additional transportation, excessive motion, greater waiting time. If occasionally a defect appears in overproduction the team must rework more units.

High level of inventory will hide many of problem areas within the organization therefore focus should be only on how to make what is required and when it is required. Lean production relies on the "Just in time" principle meaning your product should be created at the time it is required and not before.

2. Inventory

Inventory waste refers to the waste produced by unprocessed inventory. Excessive inventory is often the result of firm holding "just in case inventory" during which companies overstock themselves to meet unexpected demand, protect from production delays and low quality. Excess inventory results in waste of the storage, waste of capital tied up with unprocessed inventory, waste of transporting the inventory. The environmental impacts of inventory waste are packing, deterioration or damaged to work in process, additional materials to replace damaged or obsolete inventory as well as inventory space. However, these excessive inventories often don't meet customer's needs and don't add value. They only increase storage and depreciation costs

3.

Motion

Wasteful motion is all the motion, whether by a person or a machine, that could be minimized. If excess motion is used to add value that could have been added by less, than that margin of motion is wasted. Motion could refer to anything from a worker bending over to pick something up on the factory floor to additional wear and tear on machines, resulting in capital depreciation that must be replaced. This kind of waste includes movements of employees (or machinery), which are complicated and unnecessary. They can cause injuries, extended production time, and more. In other words, do whatever is necessary to arrange a process where workers need to do as little as possible to finish their job. Excessive travel between work stations, excessive machine movements from start point to work start point are all examples of the waste of Motion.

4. Waiting

Waiting refers to wasted time because of slowed or halted production in one step of the production chain while a previous step is completed. Whenever goods or tasks are not moving, the "waiting waste" occurs. It is easily identifiable because lost time is the most obvious thing you can detect. For example, goods waiting to be delivered, equipment waiting to be fixed, or a document waiting for executives' approval. The waste of waiting includes any idle time caused by the asynchrony of two or more interdependent processes. Operators and equipment at one step of the process end up at a standstill waiting for the second process to catch up. This will frequently happen when one process along the production line takes longer than it needs to, it results in wasted worker time. Employees can be paid when not being productive and materials can spoil when waiting for production.

5.

Defects

Defects refer to a product deviating from the standards of its design or from the customer's expectation. Defective products must be replaced; they require paperwork and human labor to process it; they might potentially lose customers; the resources put into the defective product are wasted because the product is not used. Moreover, a defective product implies waste at other levels that may have led to the defect to begin with; making a more efficient production system reduces defects and increases the resources needed to address them in the first place. Defects can cause rework, or even worse, they can lead to scrap. Usually, defective work should go back to production again, which costs valuable time. Moreover, in some cases, an extra reworking area is required, which comes with additional exploitation of labor and tools. The waste of defects includes quality errors that invariably cost you much more than you expect, as each defective product necessitates more work or replacement, wasting resources and materials, and can lead to lost customers. The environmental impact comes from the wasted labor and energy from lighting, heating, or cooling during the waiting period. Additionally, material can be spoiled, and components could be damaged because of an inefficient workflow.

6.

Overprocessing

Over-processing refers to any component of the process of manufacture that is unnecessary. This type of waste usually reflects on doing work that doesn't bring additional value, or it brings more value than required. Such things can be adding extra features to a given product that nobody will use, but they increase business costs. The environmental impact involves the excess of parts, labor, and raw materials consumed in production. Time, energy, and emissions are wasted when they are used to produce something that is unnecessary in a product; simplification and efficiency reduce these wastes and benefit the company and the environment.

7.

Transportation

Transport is moving materials from one position to another. The transport itself adds no value to the product, so minimizing these costs is essential. This means having one plant closer to another in the production chain or minimizing the costs of transportation using more efficient methods. Resources and time are used in handling material, employing staff to operate transportation, training, implement safety precautions, and using extra space. This type of waste is when you move resources (materials), and the movement doesn't add value to the product. Excessive movement of materials can be costly to your business and cause damage to quality. Often, transportation may force you to pay additionally for time, space, and machinery. Transportation waste is the movement of materials that does not directly correspond to some value-adding process. This can be very costly for your business, as you must pay for the time and machines involved in this wasteful process. It should be minimized to reduce delays, reduce the risk of handling-induced damage, and eliminate nonvalue added process steps and costs. Environmental costs to waiting include gas emissions, transportation packaging used, possible damage to the product as well as a whole host of other wastes involving transporting hazardous materials.

Value flow analysis

Over these few decades Lean" approach has been applied more than frequent in many manufacturing managements floors. Started in the automotive industry, sequential improvement initiatives were implemented to enhance the manufacturing practice changes. Value Stream Mapping (VSM) is one of the key lean tools used to identify the opportunities for various lean techniques.

The Value Flow Analysis (VFA) represents a Key Performance Indicators (KPIs) selection technique, focused on analyzing the value generated by a system at all stages: Input, Process, Output and Outcome. This technique is mostly used during the KPI selection workshop, to properly measure the value generated within each stage. For each objective, KPIs are selected for Input, Process, Output and Outcome. Based on this initial listing, the KPIs that best reflect the achievement of the objective are selected.

Input metrics are used to measure the quantity / quality of the resources provided for specific projects / activities. They usually reflect the budgets and human resource allocated, as well as the assets used.

Process metrics reflect the transformations that take place with the inputs provided, to obtain the desired outputs. At this stage, time, utilization, and availability are the key areas under surveillance.

Output metrics indicate the results obtained, usually goods or services, using inputs.

Outcome metrics are used to measure the impact of employing the goods and services (outputs) previously obtained.

The benefit of grouping KPIs within each value generation stage is that it provides a better understanding of the actual process that takes place to achieve the selected objective, and its specific phases that need to be followed. Furthermore, it offers clarity around how to achieve effectiveness and efficiency. Outcomes are compared to the desired results, thus providing the effectiveness side, while outputs are linked to the inputs used, reflecting efficiency. It is not enough to obtain the results wanted. The challenge is to achieve them with a minimum use of resources.

For a better understanding of this technique, let's take the following example: the Health Ministry sets as an objective for 2015 to lower the mortality rate in the state. The metrics assigned for each stage will be:

Input: $ Budget, # Doctors.

Process: % On-time delivery of vaccination programs.

Outputs: # Citizens vaccinated.

Outcome: % Mortality rate, % Incidence of disease.

As we can see, money and human resources were invested to make sure vaccinations will be delivered on time to the population. As a result, a certain number of citizens were vaccinated, representing the output of the vaccination process. Finally, the outcome measures the extent to which the objective was achieved. Thus, the fact that citizens were vaccinated does not reflect whether they are healthier or not. To measure that, we have to check if the incidence of disease decreased, and the mortality rates lowered. Only at that point, we can measure the extent to which the objective set was achieved.

The VFA technique is a one of the most useful approaches of identifying the most suitable KPIs for the established objectives. It is one of the most effective techniques used during KPI selection workshops, as it provides users a proper understanding of the selection process

Value added flow analysis

Value-Added Flow Analysis combines two powerful tools into one. The Value Analysis differentiates steps that add value in the eyes of the customer from those that do not, and Flow Analysis calculates the time spent on each step. This makes clear the time and effort being spent on non-value adding activities, the cost of doing business, and sets the stage for reducing waste and streamlining the process.

Guiding Principles for Lean Flow Processes

Lean discipline focuses on the objective of improving the current flow of materials, time and communication of data–by evaluating the values added to each process. That way, the areas and instances where wastes occur can be pinpointed and eliminated for purposes of process improvement.

1. Comprehend that the amount of time it takes to complete each step equates to labor cost, which the customer will pay in terms of product price. Hence fewer man-hours spent to perform a process means less value added to the product's selling price.

- Aim to identify the stage when the period allotted could be shortened by the idle time. Determine idle time as that which elapsed but did not bring any changes in the material processed.
- Analyse the time schedules of those involved in the production stages by looking at the whole block instead of focusing on a single step.
- Analyse idle time and how it can be utilized to finish the entire process. It would also be advantageous to review individual skills and the ability to perform other types of tasks.

2. Study the smoothness of the flow, which denotes that there is less time spent to move materials or equipment. Lean flow is all about finishing a task in the shortest time possible without affecting or hampering the main line of work.

- Consider the workspace and the time it takes to gather and transfer a finished batch on to the next workstation. Count the number of times that counting, bundling, and transferring each batch happen in the entire production stage.
- Study the floor plan of the working area and how workstations can be best arranged with the objective of eliminating transfer tasks.
- Eliminate time spent waiting for a batch to be completed before proceeding.

3. Make sure work performed is not duplicated, which most workers are constrained to do if the finished goods fail to meet quality control inspection.

- Establish critical points where quality should be pre-inspected before proceeding to the next processing stage. Reducing time to unravel and redo work that does not meet the standards likewise reduces time wasted for performing work on a product that will eventually fail to pass quality inspection.

4. Understand the principle of "pull-through" processes as a better alternative to "push-through" procedures. This means there is less needed to communicate by harnessing the efficiency of automation.

- Evaluate the cost of investing on software for virtual designs and automated calculations, as well as CAD (computer-aided design) or CAM (computer-aided manufacturing) equipment.
- Consider the possibility of achieving zero-errors through the help of computer technology.
- Calculate the speed and accuracy with which tasks can be accomplished in greater quantities.

Muda, Mura and Muri

Muda, mura and muri are three types of wasteful actions that negatively impact workflow, productivity and ultimately, customer satisfaction. The terms are Japanese and play an important role in the Toyato production system. The three enemies of lean can be found in both production and office processes. They can be found more in office processes than in production processes. One reason for this is that production processes are visible. Everybody who walks through a factory can see the inventory waiting to be worked on. In the office environment however, processes are often hidden inside our computers, in mailboxes and IT-systems.

Graphical user interface, website Description automatically generated

Muda, mura and muri provide guidelines for what to avoid in the way of inefficient resource allocation. Recognizing the three types of inefficiencies helps to avoid wasted time, materials, product, and human effort.

Muda means wastefulness. Work that does not add value is divided into two categories: work that is necessary but not recognized by the customer as adding value -- and work that simply is not necessary. The second type of Muda should be identified and eliminated. There are seven wastes recognized in Muda.

Mura means irregularity or a lack of uniformity. Mura is seen to cause Muda. The irregularity in production can result in lost product and wasted time. Under both the Toyota Production System and lean production, Mura should be avoided by selectively adding capacity or otherwise levelling the workload in the production line.

Muri means over worked. Pushing beyond rational workloads can be caused by Mura or by excess removal of Muda. When people or equipment are overworked, they are more prone to failure. In the case of over-worked employees, this can result in reduced productivity, absenteeism, and churn.

Muda, Mura, and Muri in Conjunction

A simple illustration shows how muda, mura, and muri often are related so that eliminating one also eliminates the others.

Suppose that a firm needs to transport six tons of material to its customer and is considering its options. One is to pile all six tons on one truck and make a single trip. But this would be muri because it would overburden the truck (rated for only three tons) leading to breakdowns, which also would lead to muda and mura.

A second option is to make two trips, one with four tons and the other with two. But this would be mura because the unevenness of materials arriving at the customer would create jam-ups on the receiving dock followed by too little work. This option also would create muri, because on one trip the truck still is overburdened, and muda as well, because the uneven pace of work would cause the waste of waiting by the customer's receiving employees.

A third option is to load two tons on the truck and make three trips. But this would be muda, even if not mura and muri, because the truck would be only partially loaded on each trip.

The only way to eliminate muda, mura, and muri is to load the truck with three tons (its rated capacity) and make two trips.

Meeting the stake holders' requirements

A stakeholder is anyone who is likely to be impacted by a project. Broadly, stakeholders can be classified into "Internal Stakeholders" and "External Stakeholders".

Internal stakeholders are within your organization. They include your Project sponsor, Project owner, Project team, any person or team who gives inputs for the project or is benefitted by the outcome of the project. It also includes those who may be impacted negatively due to the project. Example Some people who may have to re-skill due to automation or may have to be moved out.

External stakeholders are outside your organization. These could be your vendors, customers, shareholders, Government, auditors, etc. stakeholders are the lifeblood of various companies since their direct or indirect participation influences performance levels. Company includes employees, employers, customers, suppliers, distributors and investors. These stakeholders have varied needs and expectations that must be met adequately to attain their confidence and to ensure that their input is of optimal standards. Employees who form crucial stakeholders that foster service delivery expect fair treatment. They expect to receive fair remuneration, work under favorable conditions, be allocated fair duties and work for recommended hours. They also expect to be recognized, motivated, included in decision making and exposed to conventional best practices. These expectations must be met to aid their exemplary performance and their output capacity. Secondly, customers are key stakeholders who are the buyers and consumers of various products that various institutions offer. They expect to receive quality, timely and customized services at favorable prices. They are also concerned about the continuity of an institution and its efficiency in dealing with client's issues. Suppliers and distributors who ensure that raw material and finished products are delivered to respective centers are also important in a business setting. They expect to operate under mutual conditions with the management, receive their payments promptly and acquire constant feedback information from the management. Further, investors form key stakeholders whose indirect role is essential in propelling a company to greater heights. They are the ones who provide or inject finance that aids operations in most corporations. They expect a company to utilize the resources well, ensure continuity in terms of operations, production of quality products and high return on investment.

Methods of meeting stakeholder expectations or requirements

In addressing the expectations of employees, managers should put in place favourable operating policies that create good working conditions. They should pay the employees well, guarantee them safety at work, motivate them and involve them in decision making. This will boost employees' morale and enhance their output levels that are significant in the realization of quality products. Secondly, meeting the expectations of customers requires production of quality goods or services, effective delivery and adoption of favorable prices for various products.

Variably, a company that seeks to meet the expectations of distributors, suppliers and investors should put measures that promote effective communication, payment for services and financial management. The measures should also enhance or promote high return on investment and guarantee continuity in terms of operations or general performance.

Methods of communicating stakeholders' requirements with team members

Effective communication is a paramount element that any institution that seeks to address the requirements of stakeholders must ensure. This is important since communication ensures proper conveyance of organizational strategies and stakeholder needs. Company should adopt both internal and external communication methods that are able to provide quality link between the management and various stakeholders. The two probable communication methods that the companies should adopt include the use of memos for internal communication and internet.

In particular, the use of memos will ensure that the management is able to convey crucial massages pertaining to stakeholder needs for implementation by the staff members. It holds the capacity of enabling employees to know what other stakeholders needs and expectations are especially customers. This helps in ensuring that they receive adequate and satisfactory services with limited discrimination. Consequently, the technique holds the capacity of promoting effective communication under mutual terms between employers, managers and employees regarding the issues that relate to their conditions of work. It ensures that internal affairs that may jeopardize service delivery are dealt with amicably with limited complications

Secondly, the use of internet is effective for aiding both internal and external engagement or sharing of ideas. It is the latest technique that provides conventional communication support system that is effective and efficient. It links various stakeholders irrespective of location or otherwise. Indeed, it is the best method that external stakeholders can use to channel their needs or make their expectations known. This has been effective in most institutions since managers have been able to receive information from stakeholders pertaining to their needs and make requisite plans to actualize the requirements.

Processes for updating information on stakeholder requirements

The process of updating information that is obtained from stakeholders or disseminated for implementation by relevant business units must be systematic. This is to ensure that any update made is consistent to the organizational ideals and stakeholder. Evidently, updating of information of any nature is undertaken by the management. This is because they are the ones who are charged with the responsibility of receiving and coordinating various activities the institution. They are also the ones to make any possible changes to guarantee the authenticity of the information. Although the institution has information and public relations department, the department operate under the general manager. The department has the capacity to receive and prepare certain communications to various stakeholders, but dissemination of any information cannot be done without the knowledge of the managers.

Questions

1. Explain about the Lean concept?
2. How lean management has been evolved and explain about the history of lean management
3. What are the principles on which lean management can be executed?
4. What are the benefits of lean management?
5. What are the elements of Lean management?
6. Briefly discuss about seven wastes.
7. How value flow analysis improves the productivity of a manufacturing unit.
8. Describe Muda, Muri and Mura concepts?
9. Who are called as stake holders and what will be the requirements of these stake holders?

References

1. A.R. Rahani, Muhammad al-Ashraf, Production Flow Analysis through Value Stream Mapping: A Lean Manufacturing Process Case Study, Procedia Engineering, Volume 41, 2012, Pages 1727-1734,
2. Panneman, T, 2017, Lean Transformations - when and how to climb the four steps of Lean maturity, Maarssen (NL): panview

3. Panneman, T., 2019, Sustainable 5S - How to Use the lean Starting Tool, Tool to Improve Flow, Productivity and Employee Satisfaction, Dublin: Muda Masters
4. Pedro José Martínez-Jurado, José Moyano-Fuentes, Lean Management, Supply Chain Management and Sustainability: A Literature Review, Journal of Cleaner Production, Volume 85, 2014, Pages 134-150.
5. Wiggin, H., Harrington, H. J., Charron, R., Voehl, F. (2014). The Lean Management Systems Handbook. United Kingdom: Taylor & Francis.
6. Jaroslava Kadarova, Michal Demecko, New Approaches in Lean Management, Procedia Economics and Finance, Volume 39, 2016, Pages 11-16
7. Jackson, T. L., Jones, K. R. (1996). Implementing a Lean Management System. United Kingdom: Taylor & Francis.
8. Jiju Antony, Vikas Swarnakar, Elizabeth Cudney, Matthew Pepper. (2021) A meta-analytic investigation of lean practices and their impact on organisational performance. *Total Quality Management & Business Excellence* 0:0, pages 1-27.
9. Jiju Antony, Evangelos Psomas, Jose Arturo Garza-Reyes, Peter Hines. (2021) Practical implications and future research agenda of lean manufacturing: a systematic literature review. *Production Planning & Control* 32:11, pages 889-925.
10. Chao-chao Liu, Zhan-wen Niu, Qing-lin Li. (2020) The impact of lean practices on performance: based on meta-analysis and Bayesian network. *Total Quality Management & Business Excellence* 31:11-12, pages 1225-1242.
11. Shuwei Jing, Zih-Ping Ho, Zhanwen Niu. (2017) A term mining approach of interview case study on enterprise lean production. *Total Quality Management & Business Excellence* 28:11-12, pages 1414-1420.
12. Maurizio Bevilacqua, Filippo Emanuele Ciarapica, Ilaria De Sanctis. (2017) Lean practices implementation and their relationships with operational responsiveness and company performance: an Italian study. *International Journal of Production Research* 55:3, pages 769-794.

CHAPTER II

Lean tools and Techniques

Lean tools and Techniques

- Various tools of lean management
- Impact of Seiri Seiton Seiso Seiketsu and Shitsuke
- TPM (Total productive Management)
    - Need for TPM
    - TPM Pillars
    - Implementation of TPM
- OEE (Overall equipment effectiveness)
- Fundamental blocks of lean manufacturing

Lean manufacturing uses many lean tools to improve production and efficiency by getting the most out of each resource. The goal of lean manufacturing is to find better ways to do things: requiring less effort, less time, and fewer resources. Some lean tools may be more appropriate for one business than another. Organizations of all sizes are constantly looking to make their processes more efficient to remain competitive. This is where lean management tools play a significant role. With the increased elimination of waste in each process and system, Lean manufacturing helps organizations to improve continuously. Lean management tools allow a variety of manufacturers and organizations to streamline their production lines and services. These tools address different needs. They can vary from managing people to structuring work more efficiently.

Various tools of lean management

There are many different lean manufacturing tools that you can implement within your business. Together they form one comprehensive whole that can be implemented as Lean within your company. These tools are most effective if they are implemented together, however many can be used on their own to solve specific issues within your business. Lean management tools can and are used in various industries including manufacturing, engineering, and finance. Lean management tools and techniques essentially eliminate any invaluable processes, which makes them relevant to any business looking to increase their efficiency.

Here is a lean management tools list that highlights the best of the lean principles and methodology.

5S 1

Five S is mainly a management tool that is used in physical production operations. This tool aims to increase efficiency, maintain organisation, and reduce waste. It refers to a set of practices that establish order and purposefulness.

Like most Lean practices, the 5S method also began in Japan. The tool includes five terms, which are workplace practices that allow for lean production. The five terms are:

The term 5S comes from five Japanese words:

- Seiri
- Seiton
- Seiso
- Seiketsu
- Shitsuke

In English, these words are often translated to:

- Sort
- Set in Order
- Shine
- Standardize
- Sustain

Each S represents one part of a five-step process that can improve the overall function of a business.

The Origins of 5S

5S began as part of the Toyota Production System (TPS), the manufacturing method begun by leaders at the Toyota Motor Company in the early and mid-20th century. This system, often referred to as Lean manufacturing in the West, aims to increase the value of products or services for customers. This is often accomplished by finding and eliminating waste from production processes. 5S is considered a foundational part of the Toyota Production System because until the workplace is in a clean, organized state, achieving consistently good results is difficult. A messy, cluttered space can lead to mistakes, slowdowns in production, and even accidents, all of which interrupt operations and negatively impact a company.

By having a systematically organized facility, a company increases the likelihood that production will occur exactly as it should.

- Seiri: This principle refers to the separation of the needed from the unneeded items. These can include tools, parts, materials, and paperwork. The unneeded should be discarded.

The first step of 5S, Sort, involves going through all the tools, furniture, materials, equipment, etc. in a work area to determine what needs to be present and what can be removed. Some questions to ask during this phase are What is the purpose of this item? When was this item last used? How frequently is it used? Who uses it? Does it really need to be here? These questions help determine the value of each item. A workspace might be better off without unnecessary items or items used infrequently. These things can get in the way or take up space. the best people to assess the items in a space are the people who work in that space. They are the ones who can answer the above questions.

When a group has determined that some items aren't necessary, consider the following options:

- Give the items to a different department
- Recycle/throw away/sell the items
- Put items into storage

For cases when an item's value is uncertain—for example, a tool hasn't been used recently, but someone thinks it might be needed in the future—use the **red tag** method. Red tags are usually cardboard tags or stickers that can be attached to the items in question. Users fill out information about the item such as: Location, Description, Name of person applying the tag, Date of application.

Then the item is placed in a "red tag area" with other questionable items. If after a designated amount of time (perhaps a month or two) the item hasn't been used, it's time to remove it from the workspace. It's not worth hanging onto things that never get used since they just take up space.

Seiton: Whatever remaining items are left must be arranged neatly. All items must have a place and every item must stay in its place.

Set in order: Once the extra clutter is gone, it's easier to see what's what. Now work groups can come up with their own strategies for sorting through the remaining items. Things to consider: Which people (or workstations) use which items? When are items used? Which items are used most frequently? Should items be grouped by type? Where would it be most logical to place items? Would some placements be more ergonomic for workers than others? Would some placements cut down on unnecessary motion? Are more storage containers necessary to keep things organized?

During this phase, everyone should determine what arrangements are most logical. That will require thinking through tasks, the frequency of those tasks, the paths people take through the space, etc. Businesses may want to stop and think about the relationship between organization and larger Lean efforts. What arrangement will cause the least amount of waste?

In Lean manufacturing, waste can take the form of:

- Defects
- Waiting time
- Extra motion
- Excess inventory
- Overproduction
- Extra processing
- Unnecessary transportation
- Unutilized talents

Seiso: The workplace must be kept clean and free from dirt, garbage, and dust.

Shine: Everyone thinks they know what housekeeping is, but it's one of the easiest things to overlook, especially when work gets busy. The Shine stage of 5S focuses on cleaning up the work area, which means sweeping, mopping, dusting, wiping down surfaces, putting tools and materials away, etc. In addition to basic cleaning, Shine also involves performing regular maintenance on equipment and machinery. Planning for maintenance ahead of time means businesses can catch problems and prevent breakdowns. That means less wasted time and no loss of profits related to work stoppages.

Shining the workplace might not sound exciting, but it's important. And it shouldn't just be left up to the janitorial staff. In 5S, everyone takes responsibility for cleaning up their workspace, ideally on a daily basis. Doing so makes people take ownership of the space, which in the long run means people will be more invested in their work and in the company.

Seiketsu: The workplace must have established standards that must be adhered to. The best practices must be standardised through visual management.

Standardize: Once the first three steps of 5S are completed, things should look pretty good. All the extra stuff is gone, everything is organized, spaces are cleaned, and equipment is in good working order. The problem is, when 5S is new at a company, it's easy to clean and get organized and then slowly let things slide back to the way they were. Standardize makes 5S different from the typical spring-cleaning project. Standardize systematizes everything that just happened and turns one-time efforts into habits. Standardize assigns regular tasks, creates schedules, and posts instructions so these activities become routines. It makes standard operating procedures for 5S so that orderliness doesn't fall by the wayside. Depending on the workspace, a daily 5S checklist or a chart might be useful. A posted schedule indicating how frequently certain cleaning tasks must occur and who is responsible for them is another helpful tool. Initially, people will probably need reminders about 5S. Small amounts of time may need to be set aside daily for 5S tasks. But over time, tasks will become routine and 5S organizing and cleaning will become a part of regular work.

Shitsuke: Habits and behaviours must be established and implemented to ensure the established standards are maintained long-term.

Sustain: Once standard procedures for 5S are in place, businesses must perform the ongoing work of maintaining those procedures and updating them as necessary. Sustain refers to the process of keeping 5S running smoothly, but also of keeping everyone in the organization involved. Managers need to participate, as do employees out on the manufacturing floor, in the warehouse, or in the office. Sustain is about making 5S a long-term program, not just an event or short-term project. Ideally, 5S becomes a part of an organization's culture. And when 5S is sustained over time, that's when businesses will start to notice continuous positive results.

Getting Started with 5S

Even though 5S is a simple concept, beginning a new 5S program can feel daunting. It's like undertaking a big cleaning project in the garage or the basement at home; there's a lot of stuff to deal with and getting started probably doesn't sound fun. Start with practical steps such as deciding which departments and individuals will be involved, what training is needed, and what tools to use to facilitate the process. Determining these concrete things will help begin the process of 5S implementation.

Who should participate in 5 S?

Everyone, if a department is starting 5S, managers and all other employees should be included. If anyone is left out, this could lead to confusion or to messes that people don't want to take ownership of. It is possible that some people will play a bigger role in 5S than others, which is fine. There might be 5S coordinators who oversee installing and maintaining 5S labeling, keeping tracking of assigned tasks, or introducing new department members to the 5S system. These people will obviously spend a lot of time thinking about 5S compared to others. Everyone should think about 5S regularly, though. 5S might initially take place as an event, but ideally it becomes a part of daily work for everyone. It's also important to remember that company leaders should participate in 5S, especially if 5S is a company-wide effort. When people see their superiors taking 5S seriously by participating in it, they'll be more likely to take it seriously, too.

Total Productive Maintenance (TPM)

TPM (Total Productive Maintenance) is a holistic approach to equipment maintenance that strives to achieve perfect production. TPM emphasizes proactive and preventative maintenance to maximize the operational efficiency of equipment. It blurs the distinction between the roles of production and maintenance by placing a strong emphasis on empowering operators to help maintain their equipment. The implementation of a TPM program creates a shared responsibility for equipment that encourages greater involvement by plant floor workers. In the right environment this can be very effective in improving productivity.

Total Productive Maintenance is defined as a proactive approach to maintenance that aims to maximize equipment efficiency. As mentioned, this strategy is an extension of 5S that builds on the foundation of a well-organized work environment by adding well-functioning equipment into the fold. TPM isn't just a maintenance initiative, though—it's a Lean methodology that aims to establish shared responsibility for caring for equipment. Learning to work together to care for equipment can boost morale and improve collaboration across all levels of an organization. TPM also helps reduce waste, improve quality of work, and prevent costly downtime

Benefits of Total Productive Maintenance (TPM)

Going from reactive to predictive maintenance is one of the biggest advantages of implementing a TPM program. Reactive maintenance or "firefighting" is costly, as you're not only footing the bill for machinery repairs but also dealing with the cost of unplanned downtime. Let's look at some of the direct and indirect benefits that result from total productive maintenance.

Benefits of Total Productive Maintenance

Direct Benefits

Indirect Benefits

Less unplanned downtime resulting in an increase in OEE

Increase in employee confidence levels

Reduction in customer complaints

Produces a clean, orderly workplace

Reduction in workplace accidents

Increase in positive attitudes among employees through a sense of ownership

Reduction in manufacturing costs

Pollution control measures are followed

Increase in product quality

Cross-departmental shared knowledge and experience

The eight pillars of Total productive maintenance (TPM)

Traditional total productive maintenance was developed by Seiichi Nakajima of Japan. The results of his work on the subject led to the TPM process in the late 1960s and early 1970s. Nippon Denso (now Denso), a company that created parts for Toyota, was one of the first organizations to implement a TPM program. This resulted in an internationally accepted benchmark for how to implement TPM. Incorporating lean manufacturing techniques, TPM is built on eight pillars based on the 5-S system.

8 Pillars of Total Productive Maintenance

The eight pillars of total productive maintenance focus on proactive and preventive techniques to help improve equipment reliability. The eight pillars are: autonomous maintenance; focused improvement (kaizen); planned maintenance; quality management; early equipment management; training and education; safety, health and environment; and TPM in administration. Let's break down each pillar below.

1. **Autonomous maintenance:** Autonomous maintenance means ensuring your operators are fully trained on routine maintenance like cleaning, lubricating and inspecting, as well as placing that responsibility solely in their hands. This gives machine operators a feeling of ownership of their equipment and increases their knowledge of the particular piece of equipment. It also guarantees the machinery is always clean and lubricated, helps identify issues before they become failures, and frees up maintenance staff for higher-level tasks.

Implementing autonomous maintenance involves cleaning the machine to a "baseline" standard that the operator must maintain. This includes training the operator on technical skills for conducting a routine inspection based on the machine's manual. Once trained, the operator sets his or her own autonomous inspection schedule. Standardization ensures everyone follows the same procedures and processes.

1. **Focused improvement:** Focused improvement is based around the Japanese term "kaizen," meaning "improvement." In manufacturing, kaizen requires improving functions and processes continually. Focused improvement looks at the process as a whole and brainstorms ideas for how to improve it. Getting small teams in the mindset of proactively working together to implement regular, incremental improvements to processes pertaining to equipment operation is key for TPM. Diversifying team members allows for the identification of recurring problems through cross-functional brainstorming. It also combines input from across the company so teams can see how processes affect different departments.

In addition, focused improvement increases efficiency by reducing product defects and the number of processes while enhancing safety by analyzing the risks of each individual action. Finally, focused improvement ensures improvements are standardized, making them repeatable and sustainable.

3. **Planned maintenance:** Planned maintenance involves studying metrics like failure rates and historical downtime and then scheduling maintenance tasks based around these predicted or measured failure rates or downtime periods. In other words, since there is a specific time to perform maintenance on equipment, you can schedule maintenance around the time when equipment is idle or producing at low capacity, rarely interrupting production.

Additionally, planned maintenance allows for inventory buildup for when scheduled maintenance occurs. Since you'll know when each piece of equipment is scheduled for maintenance activities, having this inventory buildup ensures any decrease in production due to maintenance is mitigated.

Taking this proactive approach greatly reduces the amount of unplanned downtime by allowing for most maintenance to be planned for times when machinery is not scheduled for production. It also lets you plan inventory more thoroughly by giving you the ability to better control parts that are prone to wear and failure. Other benefits include a gradual decrease in breakdowns leading to uptime and a reduction in capital investments in equipment since it is being used to its maximum potential.

4. **Quality maintenance:** All the maintenance planning and strategizing in the world is all for naught if the quality of the maintenance being performed is inadequate. The quality maintenance pillar focuses on working design error detection and prevention into the production process. It does this by using root cause analysis (specifically the "5 Whys") to identify and eliminate recurring sources of defects. By proactively detecting the source of errors or defects, processes become more reliable, producing products with the right specifications the first time.

Possibly the biggest benefit of quality maintenance is it prevents defected products from moving down the line, which could lead to a lot of rework. With targeted quality maintenance, quality issues are addressed, and permanent countermeasures are put in place, minimizing or completely eliminating defects and downtime related to defected products.

5. **Early equipment management:** The TPM pillar of early equipment management takes the practical knowledge and overall understanding of manufacturing equipment acquired through total productive maintenance and uses it to improve the design of new equipment. Designing equipment with the input of people who use it most allows suppliers to improve maintainability and the way in which the machine operates in future designs.

When discussing the design of equipment, it's important to talk about things like the ease of cleaning and lubrication, accessibility of parts, ergonomically placing controls in a way that is comfortable for the operator, how changeovers occur and safety features. Taking this approach increases efficiency even more because new equipment already meets the desired specifications and has fewer startup issues, therefore reaching planned performance levels quicker.

6. **Training and education:** Lack of knowledge about equipment can derail a TPM program. Training and education applies to operators, managers and maintenance personnel. They are intended to ensure everyone is on the same page with the TPM process and to address any knowledge gaps so TPM goals are achievable. This is where operators learn skills to proactively maintain equipment and identify emerging problems. The maintenance team learns how to implement a proactive and preventive maintenance schedule, and managers become well-versed in TPM principles, employee development and coaching. Using tools like single-point lessons posted on or near equipment can further help train operators on operating procedures.
7. **Safety, health and environment:** Maintaining a safe working environment means employees can perform their tasks in a safe place without health risks. It's important to produce an environment that makes production more efficient, but it should not be at the risk of an employee's safety and health. To achieve this, any solutions introduced in the TPM process should always consider safety, health and the environment.

Aside from the obvious benefits, when employees come to work in a safe environment each day, their attitude tends to be better, since they don't have to worry about this significant aspect. This can increase productivity in a noticeable manner. Considering safety should be especially prevalent during the early equipment management stage of the TPM process.

8. **TPM in administration:** A good TPM program is only as good as the sum of its parts. Total productive maintenance should look beyond the plant floor by addressing and eliminating areas of waste in administrative functions. This means supporting production by improving things like order processing, procurement and scheduling. Administrative functions are often the first step in the entire manufacturing process, so it's important they are streamlined and waste-free. For example, if order-processing procedures become more streamlined, then material gets to the plant floor quicker and with fewer errors, eliminating potential downtime while missing parts are tracked down.

How to Implement Total Productive Maintenance (TPM)

Now that you have an understanding of the foundation (5-S system) and pillars on which the TPM process is built, let's take a look at how to implement a TPM program. This is generally done in five steps: identifying a pilot area, restoring equipment to prime operating condition, measuring OEE, addressing and reducing major losses, and implementing planned maintenance.

Total Productive Maintenance 5 steps

Step 1: Identify a Pilot Area

Using a pilot area to begin implementation helps gain more acceptance from staff when they see the benefits that come out of the process. When choosing equipment for a pilot area, consider these three questions:

- *What's the easiest to improve?* Selecting equipment that is easiest to improve gives you the chance for immediate and positive results; however, it doesn't test the TPM process as strongly as the other two options.
- *Where's the bottleneck?* Choosing equipment based on where production is clearly being held up gives you an immediate increase in total output

and provides quick payback. The downside is that employing this equipment as a pilot means you're using a critical asset as an example and risk the chance of it being offline longer than you would like.

- *What's the most problematic?* Fixing equipment that gives operators the most trouble will be well-received, strengthening support for the TPM program. However, this doesn't give you as much immediate payback as the previous approach, and it may be challenging to obtain a quick result from figuring out an unsolved problem, leading to disinterest.

If this is your first time implementing a TPM program, your best choice is typically the first approach – the easiest equipment to improve. If you have some or extensive experience with total productive maintenance, you may choose to correct the bottleneck. This is because you can build temporary stock or inventory, making sure downtime can be tolerated, which minimizes risk.

Include employees across all aspects of your business (operators, maintenance personnel, managers and administration) in the pilot selection process. It's a good idea to use a visual like a project board where you can post progress for all to see.

Step 2: Restore Equipment to Prime Operating Condition

The concept of restoring equipment to prime operating condition revolves around the 5-S system and autonomous maintenance. First, TPM participants should learn to continuously keep equipment to its original condition using the 5-S system: organize, cleanliness, orderliness, standardize and sustain. This might include:

- Photographing the area and current state of the equipment and then posting them to your project board.
- Clearing the area by removing unused tools, debris and anything that can be considered waste.
- Organizing the tools and components you use regularly (a shadow board with tool outlines is a popular option).
- Cleaning the equipment and the surrounding area thoroughly.
- Photographing the improvements of the equipment and surrounding area and then posting to the project board.
- Creating a standardized 5-S work process to maintain the continuity of this process.

- Auditing the process with lessening frequency (first daily, then weekly, etc.) to ensure the 5-S process is being followed (update the process to keep it current and relevant).

Once you've established a baseline state of the equipment, you can implement the autonomous maintenance program by training operators on how to clean equipment while inspecting it for wear and abnormalities. Creating an autonomous maintenance program also means developing a standardized way to clean, inspect and lubricate equipment correctly. Items to address during the planning period for the autonomous maintenance program include:

- Identifying and documenting inspection points, including parts that endure wear.
- Increasing visibility where possible to help with inspection while the machine is running (replacing opaque guarding with transparent guarding).
- Identifying and clearly labeling set points with their corresponding settings (most people put labels with settings directly on the equipment).
- Identifying all lubrication points and scheduling maintenance during changeovers or planned downtime (consider placing difficult-to-access lubrication points that require stopping the machine on the outside of the equipment).
- Training operators to make them aware of any emerging or potential issues so they can report them to the line supervisor.
- Creating an autonomous maintenance checklist for all operator-controlled tasks.
- Auditing the process with lessening frequency to ensure the checklist is being followed.

Step 3: Measure OEE

Step three requires you to track OEE for the target equipment, either manually or using automated software (as long as it includes code tracking for unplanned stoppage time). For details on how to calculate OEE manually, reference Reliable Plant's article on OEE. Regularly measuring OEE gives you a data-driven confirmation on whether your TPM program is working and lets you track progress over time.

Since the biggest losses in regard to equipment are the result of unplanned downtime, it's important to categorize every unplanned stoppage event. This gives you a more accurate look at where a stoppage is occurring. Include an "unknown" or "unallocated" stoppage time category for unknown causes.

It's recommended that you gather data for a minimum of two weeks to get an accurate representation of the unplanned stoppage time and a clear picture of how small stops and slow cycles impact production. Below is a simplified example of a top 5 loss chart. Each loss is categorized and is in descending order from the loss that causes the most downtime to the loss that causes the least.

Step 4: Address/Reduce Major Losses

Once you've got a data-driven snapshot of where your top losses are, it's time to address them. This step uses the previously discussed pillar of focused improvement or kaizen. To do this, put together a cross-functional team of operators, maintenance personnel and supervisors that can dissect the OEE data using root cause analysis and identify the main cause(s) of the losses. Your team's process might look something like this:

- Select a loss based on OEE and stoppage time data. This should be the biggest source of unplanned stoppage time.
- Look into the symptoms of the problem(s). Collect detailed information on symptoms like observations, physical evidence and photographic evidence. Using a fishbone diagram to track symptoms and record information while you're at the equipment is strongly recommended.
- With your team, discuss and identify potential causes of the problem(s), check the possible causes against the evidence you've gathered, and brainstorm the most effective ways to solve the issue.
- Schedule planned downtime to implement the agreed-upon fixes.
- Once the fix has been implemented, restart production and observe how effective the fix is over time. If it resolves the issue, make a note to implement the change and move onto the next cause of stoppage time. If not, gather more information and hold another brainstorming session.

Step 5: Implement Planned Maintenance

The last step of the TPM implementation process is the integration of proactive maintenance techniques into your program. This involves working off the third pillar of planned maintenance. Choose which components should receive proactive maintenance by looking at three factors: wear components, components that fail and stress points. Identifying stress points is often done by using infrared thermography and vibration analysis.

Next, use proactive maintenance intervals. These intervals are not set in stone and can be updated as needed. For wear and predicted failure-based components, establish the current wear level and then a baseline replacement interval. Once these have been determined, you can create a proactive replacement schedule of all wear- and failure-prone components. When doing this, use "run time" as opposed to "calendar time." Finally, develop a standardized process for creating work orders based on the planned maintenance schedule.

Sustaining the Improvement Achieved with Total Productive Maintenance (TPM)

Implementing a total productive maintenance program offers relatively short-term success. The trick is sustaining that success over the long term. This starts with the employees. If employees buy into the TPM program, envision the improved future of the company, and can see how this improved future benefits them, it can create a powerful sense of cohesiveness. Rewarding achievements is an excellent way to strengthen the established cohesiveness among employees.

Another way to achieve sustainable improvement with your TPM program is by having engaging, active leadership. This shows the importance of the program through not just words but actions. Engaging leadership prevents employees from slipping back into old habits and breathes new energy into the process on a regular basis.

Finally, don't overlook kaizen. Continuous improvement helps your TPM program adapt to changing environments and keeps the program from becoming stale and employees from becoming disinterested.

Overall Equipment Effectiveness (OEE)

Overall equipment effectiveness (OEE) is a term used to evaluate how efficiently a manufacturer's operation is being used. In other words, overall equipment effectiveness helps you notice a problem in your operations, identify which percentage of manufacturing time is productive and fix it while giving you a standardized gauge for tracking progress. The goal for measuring your OEE is continuous improvement.

How to Use Overall Equipment Effectiveness (OEE) to Measure Manufacturing Productivity

Overall equipment effectiveness is a powerful figure. It provides a lot of information in one number, so there are multiple ways OEE is used to measure manufacturing productivity. When calculated and interpreted correctly, it can significantly maximize your production. Overall equipment effectiveness is used as a benchmark to compare any given production to industry standards, in-house equipment or other shifts working on the same piece of equipment. Standard OEE benchmarks are as follows:

- An OEE score of 100 percent is considered perfect production, meaning you're only manufacturing quality parts as quickly as possible with no downtime.
- An OEE score of 85 percent is considered world class for discrete manufacturers and is a sought-after long-term goal.
- An OEE score of 60 percent is typical for discrete manufacturers and shows there is considerable room for improvement.
- An OEE score of 40 percent is considered low but not uncommon for manufacturers just starting to track and improve performance. In most cases, a low score can easily be improved through easy-to-apply measures.

Overall Equipment Effectiveness is not only a great tool for managers but can have a significant impact on employees working the plant floor. Plant floor metrics can include:

- **Target** - A real-time production target
- **Actual** - The actual production count
- **Efficiency** - The ratio of target to actual; the percentage of how far ahead or behind production is
- **Downtime** - This includes all unplanned stoppage time for each shift and is updated in real-time.

Overall Equipment Effectiveness: Terms to Know

Before we discuss overall equipment effectiveness further, there are some important terms to be aware of.

- **Fully Productive Time** - Production time after all losses is subtracted
- **Planned Production Time** - The total time your equipment or system is expected to produce

- **Ideal Cycle Time** - The time it takes to manufacture one part
- **Run Time** - The time your system is scheduled for production and is running
- **Total Count** - The total of all parts produced including those with defects
- **Good Count** - Parts produced that meet quality-control standards
- **Good Parts** - Parts produced that meet standards and don't need to be redone
- **Quality** - This refers to manufactured parts that don't meet quality-control standards, including ones that need to be reworked. It is calculated as *Quality = Good Count / Total Count.*
- **Performance** - This considers the number of times there are slowdowns or brief stops in production. A perfect performance score in OEE terms means your operation is running as quickly as possible. It is calculated as *Performance = (Ideal Cycle Time x Total Count) / Run Time.*
- **Availability** - This considers planned and unplanned stoppage time. A perfect availability score means your operation is constantly running during planned production times. It is calculated as *Availability = Run Time / Planned Production Time.*

How to Calculate Overall Equipment Effectiveness (OEE)

Before calculating overall equipment effectiveness, it's important to denote the difference between the terms *effectiveness* and *efficiency* when discussing OEE.

Effectiveness is the relationship between what could technically be produced and what is produced at the end of a production period. For example, if your machinery can make 100 products an hour and it only makes 80, then it is 80 percent effective.

However, this doesn't tell us how *efficient* the machinery is because we didn't consider things like the number of operators, energy and the materials needed to reach 80 percent effectiveness. For example, if your machinery runs 60 percent effective with one employee and becomes 75 percent effective with two employees, the effectiveness increases by 25 percent, but efficiency decreases to 50 percent based on labour.

There are two main ways to calculate OEE:

- **Simple Calculation:** The easiest way to calculate OEE is the ratio of fully productive time to planned production time. It looks like this: *OEE =*

(Good Count x Ideal Cycle Time) / Planned Production Time.

- **Preferred Calculation:** This type of OEE calculation is based on the three OEE factors discussed earlier – availability, performance, and quality (good count). It looks like this: *Availability x Performance x Quality = OEE*. This is the preferred calculation method because not only do you get your OEE score showing how well you're doing, but you get three numbers (availability, performance, and quality) showing what caused your losses.

Preferred Calculation Example

Below we'll look at two examples of Preferred Calculation.

Item

Data

Downtime

5%

Efficiency

96%

Quality (Yield)

98%

A widget-making machine with 5 percent downtime (or 95 percent availability) has an efficiency of 96 percent. (ASTM and other governing bodies help determine some machine efficiency ratings. For others, it's as simple as looking at that machine's specific production.) Two of every 100 widgets the machine makes are rejected as being out of specification (98 percent quality). Since OEE is calculated by multiplying the three factors (availability, performance, and quality), your formula looks like this: *OEE = 0.95 x 0.96 x 0.98 = 89.376 percent*

Let's look at a more practical example. A normal shift at a bottling facility takes 480 minutes. Machine operators take three breaks during their shift totalling 50 minutes, and they do two changeovers during the shift totalling 60 minutes of machine downtime for a total of 180 minutes of lost time. To calculate the availability part of the equation, we take:

480 minutes - 180 minutes = 300 minutes

300 minutes / 480 = **62.5 percent Availability**

To calculate the performance part of the equation, let's assume the bottling plant produces 60 bottles per minute. Factoring in the remaining 300 minutes, the bottling system can make 18,000 bottles (300 x 60). Let's say the machines are running slower at 1.5 seconds of cycle time, slowing the maximum speed by two-thirds. This reduces the actual performance to 12,000 bottles. So, to calculate the performance part of the equation, we take:

1.5 seconds per bottle = 1 / 1.5 = 2/3 = **66.7 percent Performance** (66.7 percent x 18,000 bottles = 12,000 units)

To calculate the quality part of the equation, let's say out of the 12,000 bottles, 3,000 don't meet quality-control standards, making the quality rate of the bottles 75 percent. The quality part of the equation is calculated as:

(12,000 - 3,000 defects) / 12,000 = **75 percent Quality**

Another way to look at it is 3,000 bottles / 60 bottles per minute = 50 minutes lost quality.

So, to calculate the overall equipment effectiveness (Availability x Performance x Quality = OEE), we'd take **62.5 percent x 66.7 percent x 75 percent = 31.25 percent OEE**. This means we could technically produce 28,800 bottles, but in the end, only 9,000 bottles are cleared for sale (9,000 / 28,800) = 31.25 percent.

Perhaps the biggest goal of implementing an OEE program is to reduce or eliminate the most common causes of machine- or equipment-based productivity loss, known as the six big losses. These six losses are broken down into the three main OEE categories (availability, performance, and quality).

Available Losses

1. **Equipment Failure:** This is equipment that is not running when it is scheduled for production, causing unplanned downtime. Machine breakdowns, unplanned maintenance stops, and tooling failure are common examples.
2. **Setup and Adjustments:** This is production downtime due to changeovers, machine and tooling adjustments, planned maintenance, inspections and setup/warmup time.

Performance Losses

1. **Idling and Minor Stops:** Sometimes called small stops, idling and minor stops are when equipment stops for a short period of time. This can be caused by jams, flow obstructions, wrong settings or cleaning. These issues are usually resolved by the operator.

2. **Reduced Speed:** Sometimes referred to as slow cycles, reduced speed is when equipment runs at speeds slower than the ideal cycle time (the fastest possible time). Worn out or poorly maintained equipment due to poor lubrication practices, substandard materials and bad environmental conditions are common causes of reduced speed.

Quality Losses

1. **Process Defects:** This refers to any defective part manufactured during stable production, including scrapped parts and parts that can be reworked. Incorrect machine settings and operator or equipment errors are common reasons for process defects.
2. **Reduced Yield:** Reduced yield refers to defective parts made from startup until stable production is achieved. Like process defects, this can mean scrapped parts and parts that can be reworked. Reduced yield most commonly occurs after changeovers, incorrect settings and during machine warmups.

Five Benefits of Using Overall Equipment Effectiveness (OEE) to Improve Production

Implementing an overall equipment effectiveness strategy is a powerful advantage in achieving your production targets. It allows you to take a proactive approach by tweaking manufacturing processes in real time, reducing downtime, increasing capacity, reducing costs, improving quality and increasing efficiency. Let's take a look at 10 benefits of OEE.

1. **Return of Investment (ROI) for Equipment:** Companies invest heavily in machinery, so it's important to maximize the return on this investment. If you can use an OEE strategy to produce 15 percent more product on the same equipment in the same amount of time, it can greatly impact your bottom line.
2. **Increase Competitiveness:** Manufacturers always strive to reduce losses during production to achieve maximum competitiveness. Using data from an OEE report helps you identify bottlenecks or weaknesses in production, allowing you to take immediate action.

Quality and competitiveness go together, and OEE's quality metric can help you identify problems in production causing scrap or rework parts.

3. **Cutting Machinery Costs:** An OEE strategy helps you understand your equipment's actual performance, so you know whether it is working efficiently. It also alerts you to issues that may lead to future breakdowns and repairs. Overall equipment effectiveness lets you anticipate potential machine failure, reducing maintenance costs and downtime.
4. **Maximize Workforce Productivity:** Use OEE to see why you experience operator downtime, reveal productivity data and pinpoint long changeovers or setup times. Information like this helps you appropriately allot resources, identify where excess capacity is occurring and determine where you need new hires.
5. **Easily Visualize Performance:** Overall equipment effectiveness emphasizes visibility, letting you visualize production problems instead of having to rely on your best guess. By highlighting the biggest sources of productivity losses into one single percentage, everyone can see what's working and where improvement is needed.

Questions

1. What are the various tools used in lean Management?
2. Briefly explain about 5" S?
3. Explain about TPM?
4. What are the 8 Pillars of TPM?
5. Explain the process of implementation of TPM?
6. How to Use Overall Equipment Effectiveness (OEE) to Measure Manufacturing Productivity?

References

1. Delisle, Dennis R, Freiberg, Valentina, Everything Is 5S: A Simple Yet Powerful Lean Improvement Approach Applied In A Preadmission Testing Center, Quality Management Journal, Volume 21, Issue 4, 2014, pages 10-22.
2. Davis, Scott Marchand, Office Efficiency, Quality progress, Volume 51, Issue 2, 2018, pages 16-21.
3. Jackson, T. L., Jones, K. R. (1996). Implementing a Lean Management System. United Kingdom: Taylor & Francis.

4. Mikhailovsky, P., Plakhin, A., Ogorodnikova, E., Kochergina, T., Guseva, T., & Selezneva, M. (2020). Lean management tools to improve the production system. *Calitatea, 21*(176), 65-68.
5. Parry, G. C., & Turner, C. E. (2006). Application of lean visual process management tools. *Production planning & control, 17*(1), 77-86.
6. Mann, D. (2005). *Creating a lean culture: tools to sustain lean conversions.* Productivity Press.
7. Minh, N. D. (2020). A new application model of lean management in small and medium sized enterprises.
8. Sanders, A., K Subramanian, K. R., Redlich, T., & Wulfsberg, J. P. (2017, September). Industry 4.0 and lean management–synergy or contradiction?. In *IFIP international conference on advances in production management systems* (pp. 341-349). Springer, Cham.
9. Wolniak, R. (2014). Relationships between selected lean management tools and innovations. *Zeszyty Naukowe. Organizacja i Zarządzanie/ Politechnika Śląska*, (75), 157-166.

CHAPTER III

Lean System

Lean System

- Features manufacturing and services
- Workflow
- Small lot sizes
- Pull Method
- Kanban
- A3 problem solving,
- Just In Time.

Lean System

A Lean system describes a business or business unit that holistically applies Lean principles to the way it plans, prioritizes, manages, and measures work. The goal for any Lean system is to maximize customer value. While Lean thinking can greatly improve the productivity and function of a team or department, Lean implementations that spread across the entire organization have the greatest impact on the customer.

Lean systems use a Lean approach to identify and eliminate waste. They systematically discover and act upon opportunities to improve. These are two of the fundamental concepts of Lean: Eliminate anything that does not add value to the customer, and work systematically and continuously to create more value for the customer.

Guiding Principles of a Lean System

Although transforming into a Lean system involves a great deal of effort, Lean's lightweight, flexible nature makes it easy to scale than more structured, regimented methodologies. Practicing Lean thinking begins with a thorough understanding of these 7 Lean principles.

Optimize the whole

Visualize, optimize, and manage the entire organizational value stream as one value-generating system. Make decisions that optimize the entire organization's ability to deliver value to the customer, not just one team or department.

Create knowledge

A Lean system is a learning system; it grows and develops through analyzing the results of small, incremental experiments. In order to retain the insight and knowledge gained from constant experimentation, Lean systems must provide the infrastructure necessary to properly document and retain value learnings.

Eliminate waste

Lean systems use this definition of waste: If your customer wouldn't pay for it, it's waste. Waste can be anything from context switching, to too much work in process, to time spent manually completing a task that could be automated. Lean thinkers are relentless about eliminating any process, activity, or practice that does not result in more value for the customer.

Build quality in

Lean organizations set themselves up for sustainable growth by building quality into processes and documentation. They automate and standardize any tedious, repeatable process or any process prone to human error, which allows them to error-proof significant portions of their value streams.

Deliver fast

In Lean, flow refers to the manner by which work moves through your organizational system. Good flow describes a Lean system with a steady, consistent flow of value delivery, while bad flow describes a system with unpredictable delivery and unsustainable habits.

Defer commitment

This Lean principle says that Lean systems should function as just-in-time systems, waiting until the last responsible moment to make decisions and deliver work. This is based on the idea that the longer we wait, the greater the chance that our decisions will be well-informed, based on data that reflects the reality of the market.

Respect people

At its core, all successful Lean systems are rooted in one thing: Respect for people. Lean systems are designed to maximize customer value while minimizing waste, out of respect for the customer. Out of respect for employees, Lean systems encourage environments that allow everyone to do their best work. In Lean systems, team members continuously strive to optimize processes to allow everyone to deliver the most value they can provide.

Features of manufacturing and services

The term Lean manufacturing refers to the application of Lean practices, principles, and tools to the development and manufacture of physical products. Many manufacturers are using Lean manufacturing principles to eliminate waste, optimize processes, cut costs, boost innovation, and reduce time to market in a fast-paced, volatile, ever-changing global marketplace.

For many people, the phrase "Lean manufacturing" is synonymous with removing waste – and eliminating waste is certainly a key element of any Lean practice. But the ultimate goal of practicing Lean manufacturing isn't simply to eliminate waste – it's to sustainably deliver value to the customer.

To achieve that goal, Lean manufacturing defines waste as anything that doesn't add value to the customer. This can be a process, activity, product, or service; anything that requires an investment of time, money, and talent that does not create value for the customer is waste. Idle time, underutilized talent, excess inventory, and inefficient processes are all considered waste by the Lean definition.

Lean manufacturing provides a systematic method for minimizing waste within a manufacturing system, while staying within certain margins of control such as productivity and quality. In this article, we'll discuss the:

- Origins of Lean manufacturing
- Importance of understanding Lean principles in any Lean practice
- Key concepts of modern Lean manufacturing practices

The Toyota Way includes 14 principles, which are often organized into these four main ideas:

1. Long-Term Philosophy: Make management decisions based on long-term philosophy, even at the expense of short-term financial goals.
2. The Right Process Will Produce the Right Results: A relentless emphasis on process is critical for sustainably delivering value. This means creating a continuous process flow, using a "pull" system instead of a "push" system (as we'll explain later), balancing capacity and demand, standardizing repeatable tasks and processes, and creating a culture of "stopping the line" when errors occur, so that problems can be fixed as soon as they arise.
3. Add Value to the Organization by Developing Your People: People are an organization's greatest asset. Invest in them, support them, encourage their growth, and treat them with respect by continuously working to improve the environment in which they operate. This includes employees, customers, vendors, and suppliers.

4. Continuously Solving Root Problems Drives Organizational Learning: Every "mistake" is a teachable moment. By analysing, studying, and openly discussing when and how things go wrong, organizations can learn and grow. The role of leaders is to prioritize learning over perfection – to experience and problem solve issues as they arise, and share learnings so that the same mistakes are not repeated.

All four of these concepts can be found in modern implementations of Lean manufacturing. However, throughout the twentieth century, TPS concepts were often left out as companies formed their own ideas of how Lean manufacturing could contribute to their success.

In attempts to emulate the success of Toyota, many companies translated "going Lean" to mean cutting waste, cutting corners, and cutting people: relentless elimination of waste with little regard for the health of the overall system.

Key Lean Manufacturing Concepts

Jim Womack and Dan Jones finally captured the essence of why some Lean organizations thrived while others failed. First in The Machine that Changed the World and then in Lean Thinking, they raised our level of understanding from copying specific practices to seeing the underlying principles that make the entire system work.

While you might not think of them as principles specific to Lean manufacturing, you may recognize some of these concepts from their work:

- Value stream mapping
- Demand-based (pull) system
- Continuous improvement
- Measurement, KPIs, and Visualization

These Lean manufacturing concepts and tools enable organizations to become nimbler and more innovative, while improving quality and production time.

Value stream mapping

The term "value stream" refers to the process it takes to turn a customer request into a deliverable piece of value. Value stream mapping is the analysis of that process, and can be used to improve any process where there are repeatable steps, and especially when there are multiple handoffs. The purpose of value stream mapping is to be able to analyse the overall process and each of its steps, to be able to design out (to borrow from TPS) overburden, inconsistency, and waste.

To understand the role that a value stream plays in Lean manufacturing, think of the concept of an assembly line: There are specific steps that need to be done in order for a collection of raw parts to be turned into a functional product. Mapping out this value stream involves defining each of those steps and where handoffs occur between them.

But modern manufacturing value streams are more complex, combining the work of mechanical and software engineers, scientists, chemists, designers, and others. The actual manufacture of the physical product is just one part of a much larger value stream. Defining and visualizing each of these steps is critical to practicing process improvement.

Inefficient handoffs in knowledge work may not look like bottlenecks on a car assembly line, but they produce the same effect: decreased productivity, overwhelmed workers, and lower work quality.

Analysing inefficiencies and taking steps to eliminate them at the organizational level is the first step toward becoming leaner. Lean actions can be focused on specific logistical processes, or cover the entire supply chain.

For example, an analysis of a SKU would look like this: First the path is visualized, and all the participants from material suppliers to the consumer are evaluated, before a gap analysis is conducted to determine necessary next steps to improve the value stream and achieve the objective. Then small improvements are made, over time, throughout the supply chain, increasing organizational learning and streamlining the process of creating that SKU.

Demand-based flow (pull) manufacturing

Lean manufacturing is all about optimizing flow: Creating a system that sustainably, consistently delivers value. The sustainability part of this relies on effectively managing capacity – making sure that the workload is balanced and manageable throughout the value stream. Implementing a demand-based, or (pull) manufacturing system is key to effectively managing capacity.

In a pull manufacturing system, inventory is only pulled through each production center when it is needed to meet a customer's order. Pull systems allow "just-in-time" delivery of work. Unlike other work methods that allow for an unlimited amount of work at once, a pull system enables everyone at a specific organizational level to focus on one thing (or just a few things) at one time.

Benefits of using a Kanban control system or pull system include:

- Ability to manage change
- Ability to quickly adapt work to new information
- Increased ability to scale the team to the appropriate size for the project

As they work through a list of "to-do" items in a backlog, team members pull new tasks only as old tasks are completed. This way, when something changes that impacts the business requirements (as it always does), the team can quickly adapt, knowing that the majority of work they have already completed can still be applied to the project.

Finally, because teams using a pull system are self-managed to a certain degree, pull systems contribute to the scalability of a team, or the ability for a team to accommodate different sized projects while remaining cohesive.

For manufacturers, this means teams can be more agile, deliver faster, and innovate faster and more strategically. Organizations that adopt a Lean pull system are also able to significantly improve the reliability and accuracy of forecasting for their suppliers and customers.

Continuous improvement

An organization-wide commitment to continuous improvement is essential for sustainable success with Lean manufacturing. At its core, Lean is continuous improvement – it's improving product and process while eliminating redundant, excessive, or inefficient activities.

Continuous improvement can be viewed as a formal practice or an informal set of guidelines – but it must be well integrated into the culture of an organization in order to make a meaningful and lasting difference.

Measurement, KPIs, and visualization

A famous quote by management expert and consultant Peter Drucker says, "You can't manage what you can't measure."

Lean manufacturing metrics, such as lead time, cycle time, throughput, and cumulative flow help organizations measure the impact of their improvement efforts. Collecting, analysing, visualizing, and socializing these metrics (through shared dashboards) is essential to promoting transparency and driving change.

Successful Lean manufacturers use up-to-date dashboards at the team, leader, and executive levels to paint an accurate picture of the impact that changed processes are having. It should be noted that the emphasis is on surfacing key performance indicators of processes – not people. This reinforces a collective responsibility by teams to pursue opportunities for improvement and focus on value creation for customers.

Workflow

Workflow is the series of activities that are necessary to complete a task. Each step in a workflow has a specific step before it and a specific step after it, except for the first and last steps. In a linear workflow, an outside event usually initiates the first step. If the workflow has a loop structure, however, the completion of the last step will usually restart the first step.

Tools such as flowcharts and process maps are used to visualize the steps involved in a process and the order they should go in. Flowcharts use simple geometric symbols and arrows to define if-then relationships. Process maps look similar, but they may also include support information. That information documents the resources that each step in a business process requires.

Workflow can be automated with software tools that use business rules to decide when one step has been completed successfully and the next step can begin. Some workflow management apps can also coordinate dependent relationships between individual steps, a concept known as workflow orchestration. Workflow management software also provides workflow templates for documentation and business process modelling, two important aspects of business process management (BPM).

Types of workflows

Workflows are categorized in various ways. At a basic level, they get grouped using one of these two approaches:

- **Sequential.** This type of workflow has a series of steps that happen one after the other to complete the task. A loan application approval typically follows a sequential workflow, where a step is finished before the next one starts. A rules-driven workflow is a subset; based on sequential workflow, a rules-driven workflow progresses along a sequential path based on which rules get triggered.
- **Parallel.** With this approach, a series of steps is tackled concurrently to move the task toward completion. Employee onboarding workflow often takes a parallel approach because many of the tasks required of a new hire -- from healthcare insurance enrollment to security clearances to direct deposit forms -- can happen simultaneously.

There are other ways to categorize workflows, including the following three:

- **Process workflow.** This approach is comprised of a predictable, repetitive sequence of tasks or steps.
- **Case workflow.** With these processes, the exact sequence of steps needed to complete the task are unknown at the start and can vary case by case.
- **Project workflow.** The flow of steps proceeds in a structured path similar to process workflow, but there is some flexibility in when, how and even if all those steps must happen.

More infrequently, some people categorize processes as delivery, request- or task-based workflows. A state machine workflow is another possible category. It's traditionally considered a modeling style for event-driven workflows.

Workflows are also sometimes distinguished as manual or digital. Digital workflows are usually automated workflows and ones that use artificial intelligence (AI). Manual and digital workflows are also sometimes called human-centered versus system-centered workflows, respectively.

Examples and uses of workflows

Business workflows exist in every organization across all industries. Some follow similar steps, if not identical, in many organizations. Others are unique to industries or the enterprise that's using it.

Workflows can be found in all departments and functions in an organization from product development and project management to back-office administration and front-end customer service. Some workflows are highly structured, while others are completely unstructured. Many falls between those two extremes.

Each workflow moves data from one step to the next. That's what distinguishes a workflow from a checklist, which is a collection of unrelated tasks.

A company would use a workflow to describe the process for paying an electric bill. It likely involves the following steps:

1. receiving the bill.
2. reviewing the bill.
3. approving payment; and
4. disbursing the funds for payment.

A checklist can ensure adherence to the routine for powering down all electricity in a facility at the end of a business day. That's a process that doesn't necessarily involve specific steps happening in a certain order.

Typical processes that involve workflows include the following:

- approval of employee paid time-off requests.
- billing and invoicing.
- customer onboarding;
- intake of a customer request.
- onboarding new employees.
- performance assessment.
- processing sales orders.
- product assembly.
- sales fulfillment; and
- IT help desk ticket submission.

What are the components of a workflow?

There are three basic components within every workflow:

1. **Input** is also called *start* or *trigger*. It is the information, materials and resources required to complete each step within the task.
2. **Transformation** is also referred to as *work*. It involves the actions taken to perform each step and move through the sequential or parallel steps.
3. **Output** is also called *result* or *outcome*. It is the result of each step that then becomes the input for follow-on steps within the workflow. The finished task is the final output.

How to create a workflow

Workflows exist in organizations even if they're not well-defined or managed to any degree. However, workflows that are not planned or managed often have operational inefficiencies. On the other hand, workflows that are thoughtfully created and well managed are efficient. They are also less prone to errors and likely to improve over time.

The creation of a workflow involves multiple steps, which can be depicted in a workflow diagram as a sequence of steps or written as a list of required actions.

Creating a process-improving workflow requires the following series of tasks:

1. Identify the start and endpoint of the process.
2. List or map out each step required to move from the start point to the endpoint.
3. Assess whether these tasks must happen in a specific order and, if so, list or map them accordingly.
4. Determine and document the resources and roles within the organization that are required to complete each step. Add required workflow rules or business process descriptions.
5. Execute workflow.

Most organizations use workflow management systems to set up, document and monitor workflows. These systems have libraries of prebuilt workflows and provide building blocks that businesses can use to create new workflows. Some also have AI capabilities that can identify and add efficiencies and improve business operations and processes.

What is workflow management?

Once an organization has created and documented a workflow, it must manage it as part of its overall BPM efforts. Workflow management is the discipline of creating, documenting, monitoring, and improving a workflow. This process enables organizations to optimize workflows, ensuring each step is completed correctly, consistently, and efficiently.

Workflow management also lets organizations identify and correct bottlenecks, superfluous steps, and other problems within the workflow. Many of these could slow the execution of tasks in the workflow, increase the risk of errors and require more resources than necessary to complete an activity.

When effectively implemented, workflow management can continuously improve workflows within an organization. Consequently, it saves time and money while reducing errors.

What is a workflow diagram, and who uses it?

A workflow diagram — sometimes called a process flowchart — is a graphic/visual overview of a repeatable linear process intended to see a task through to completion. Its purpose is to make complex workflows easier to understand by making them visual.

An example diagram of a content publishing workflow.

Understanding the shapes of a workflow diagram

As shown in the example above, a workflow diagram consists of various geometric shapes and arrows that help define each step further. Here's a chart to make sense of it of a basic one—you might find other variations. That's why it's important to include legends for your work processes.

workflow chart symbols

What is a Lot size?

Lot size refers to the quantity of an item ordered for delivery on a specific date or manufactured in a single production run. In other words, lot size basically refers to the total quantity of a product ordered for manufacturing. In financial markets, lot size is a measure or quantity increment suitable to or précised by the party which is offering to buy or sell it. A simple example of lot size is when we buy a pack of six chocolates, it refers to buying a single lot of chocolate.

Small Vs. Large Lot Sizes

While it's commonly understood that small and large lot sizes each have distinct advantages, how to get the best of both is not.

The choice between small and large lot sizes is best approached from a both/and perspective. But for many companies, this choice is often seen as either/or. This assumption is not always unfounded: many manufacturing partners lack the capability to deliver the best of both. The reasons for this are twofold: First, they may lack the facilities and technology. Second, they may lack the in-house DFM expertise (Design For Manufacture) that ensures an innovation is optimized for flexible and scalable manufacturing.

Let's look at the advantages of small and large lot sizes and how to get the best of both.

Small Lot Sizes

While small lot sizes have traditionally been reserved for customized or quasi-customized products, small lot sizes can sometimes make sense for "plug and play" products as well. For instance, while modular or simple products will almost always call for large lot sizes, small lots can be used for optional customization further down the chain. While it's generally more cost-effective to manufacture in large lots, small lot sizes can come with hidden benefits.

Small lots reduce excess inventory and warehouse storage costs and all but eliminate waste. They simplify scheduling and can enhance quality. Regardless of whether the product in question is MTO (Made To Order) or MTS (Make To Stock), small lots can be an essential part of lean manufacturing strategy.

Large Lot Sizes

Though large lots do not allow for customization and can come with high inventory and warehousing costs, manufacturing in bulk is highly cost-effective and the obvious choice for a wide range of consumer, industrial, and medical products. Other advantages include reduced variability and the ability to ship products on demand.

ELS (Economic Lot Size)

It's critically important to understand the various advantages afforded by small and large lot sizes; however, a bigger question needs to be addressed. This question concerns ELS (Economic Lot Size) and the flexibility and agility required for driving down COGS by scaling production in response to fluctuating demand and changing market conditions.

To illustrate, say a company forecasts product demand at 500 units for the coming year but learns that the most cost-effective lot size is 1,000. This means that two years' worth of inventory will need to be stored and managed. If market demand drops significantly in this time, the business selling this product is likely in for some serious trouble. If this business had selected a manufacturing partner that offered flexible production runs from the beginning, a drop in demand would be a far less risky proposition.

On the other hand, if you're a successful start-up company that is slowly breaking new ground, penetrating new markets, and manufacturing in small lots in response to customer demand. Suppose the product takes off and demand suddenly spikes. In that case, the start-up will need a manufacturing partner with the flexibility to increase lot size and rapidly ramp up production to capitalize on this unexpected growth opportunity.

What Is a Pull System?

A pull system is a lean manufacturing strategy used to reduce waste in the production process. In this type of system, components used in the manufacturing process are only replaced once they have been consumed so companies only make enough products to meet customer demand. This means all the company's resources are used for producing goods that will immediately be sold and return a profit.

Essentially, a pull system works backwards, starting with the customer's order then using visual signals to prompt action in each previous step in the process. The product is pulled through the manufacturing process by the consumer's demand.

Pull System vs. Push System

Another system used in supply chains is a push system, which sharply contrasts with a pull system. In a push system, units are produced based on forecasted demand and then pushed into the market, whereas a pull system uses actual demand. Companies using a push system must predict what the customer will want to purchase and in what quantity, which is difficult as sales can be unpredictable and vary from previous years.

In a pull system, the quantity produced is just enough to meet current demand. However, in a push system, products are mass produced for estimated future demand. These products must remain in inventory until they are needed, which could take months, years or may not happen at all.

Advantages Of Using a Pull System

Manufacturing facilities greatly benefit from switching from a push system to a pull system. Using a pull system reduces waste within a company since no overproduction occurs. This also frees up space in the workplace and reduces the cost of storing excess inventory.

Businesses that use a pull system experience increased customer satisfaction as products are manufactured specifically to fulfill their requests. Since products are made in small quantities, quality issues will be identified faster than with a push system and, if an error is found, less defective products would require disposal.

A pull system allows manufacturing facilities to save time that would be spent planning for future demand and producing goods that may never be sold. They also experience increased flexibility, as they can rapidly respond to changes in demand. Each of these advantages of using a pull system reduces total costs for the business, whether directly or indirectly, resulting in increased profit.

Using Kanban in a Pull System

The signals which permit production materials to be replaced or refilled are called Kanban's. Meaning "signal" in Japanese, these cues use visual communication to put a pull system into practice. A Kanban will be placed where products or manufacturing components are stored and will signal when these need to be replenished. With this process, items needed are always available and will not be replenished without a signal from further down the production process.

Kanban signals can come in many forms. Kanban cards are the most common type of signal. These cards are sent to a previous step in the manufacturing process to indicate that more products or parts are needed. However, a Kanban can be as simple as an empty container that a worker can see needs to be refilled. The Kanban will provide the worker with information for replenishing the items such as the reorder quantity and part numbers.

Kanban signals provide an effective way to implement a pull system, which will lead to an overall more organized, efficient, and profitable business. Manufacturing facilities currently using a push system should evaluate their supply chain for waste and consider switching to a pull system to experience a leaner manufacturing process.

Introduction to Kanban

Kanban is a visual system for managing work as it moves through a process. Kanban visualizes both the process (the workflow) and the actual work passing through that process. The goal of Kanban is to identify potential bottlenecks in your process and fix them so work can flow through it cost-effectively at an optimal speed or throughput.

Kanban is a popular Lean workflow management method for defining, managing, and improving services that deliver knowledge work. It helps you visualize work, maximize efficiency, and improve continuously. Work is represented on Kanban boards, allowing you to optimize work delivery across multiple teams and handle even the most complex projects in a single environment.

Kanban Definition

The Japanese word "Kanban", meaning "visual board" or a "sign", has been used in the sense of a process definition since the 1950s. It was first developed and applied by Toyota as a scheduling system for just-in-time manufacturing. On the other hand, the capitalized term "Kanban" is known and associated with the emergence of the "Kanban Method," which was first defined in 2007.

The Genesis of Kanban

Initially, it arose as a scheduling system for lean manufacturing, originating from the Toyota Production System (TPS). In the late 1940s, Toyota introduced "just in time" manufacturing to its production. The approach represents a pull system. This means that production is based on customer demand rather than the standard push practice to produce goods and push them to the market.

Their unique production system laid the foundation of Lean manufacturing or simply Lean. Its core purpose is minimizing waste activities without sacrificing productivity. The main goal is to create more value for the customer without generating more costs.

The Kanban Method

At the beginning of the 21st Century, key players in the software industry quickly realized how Kanban could positively change the way products and services were delivered.

With an increased focus on efficiency and by harnessing advances in computing technology, Kanban left the automotive industry's realm and was successfully applied to other complex commercial sectors such as IT, software development, R&D, and others.

Indeed, what we now recognize as the Kanban Method emerged at the beginning of 2007. It is a result of years of testing, experience, and joint efforts of leading figures in the Lean and Agile community such as David Aderson, Dan Vacanti, Darren Davis, Corey Ladas, Dominica DeGrandis, Rick Garber, and others.

You can start building your Kanban system by setting up the most straightforward Kanban board with three basic columns – "Requested", "In Progress" and "Done". When constructed, managed, and functioning correctly, it serves as a real-time information repository, highlighting bottlenecks within the system and anything else that might interrupt smooth working practices.

Kanban Principles

Before exploring the Kanban values in more detail, we'd like to establish that the method in the shape and form we embrace and use today emerged due to many people's collaborative efforts. The expanding Kanban community should acknowledge these ideas and contributions as such.

David J. Anderson (a pioneer in the field of Lean/ Kanban for knowledge work and one of the founding fathers of the method) has formulated the Kanban method as an approach to incremental, evolutionary process and systems change for knowledge work organizations. It is focused on getting things done, and its fundamentals can be broken down into **two types of principles and six practices.**

Let's examine what the Kanban principles are.

Change Management Principles

Service Delivery Principles

Start With What You Do Now

Focus on Customer's Needs and Expectations

Agree to Pursue Incremental, Evolutionary Change

Manage the Work, Not the Workers

Encourage Acts of Leadership at All Levels

Regularly Review the Network of Services

Change Management Principles

Blending with the already established processes in a non-disruptive way, pursuing evolutionary changes and continuous improvement. Let's take a closer look at the Kanban change management principles.

Principle 1: Start With What You Do Now

Kanban offers the flexibility to use the method on top of existing workflows, systems, and processes without disrupting what is already in place. The method recognizes that existing processes, roles, responsibilities, and titles have value and are, generally, worth preserving. Naturally, it will highlight issues that need to be addressed and help assess and plan changes so their implementation is as non-disruptive as possible.

Principle 2: Agree to Pursue Incremental, Evolutionary Change

The Kanban method is designed to meet minimal resistance. It encourages continuous small incremental and evolutionary changes to the current process by implementing collaboration and feedback forms. In general, sweeping changes are discouraged because they usually encounter resistance due to fear or uncertainty.

Principle 3: Encourage Acts of Leadership at All Levels

Leadership at all levels derives from people's everyday insights and acts to improve their way of working. As insignificant as you may think, each shared observation fosters a continuous improvement mindset (Kaizen) to reach optimal performance on a team/department/company level. This can't be a management-level activity.

Service Delivery Principles

Kanban aims at developing a service-oriented approach. It requires that you profoundly understand your customer's needs, create a network of services where people self-organize around the work, and ensure that your system continuously evolves.

Principle 1: Focus on Customer's Needs and Expectations

Delivering value to the customer should be at the centre of each organization. Understanding the needs and expectations of your customers brings the attention to the quality of the provided services and the value it creates.

Principle 2: Manage the Work

Managing the work in your network of services ensures that you empower people's abilities to self-organize around the work. This enables you to focus on the desired outcomes without the "noise" created by micro-managing the people delivering the services.

Principle 3: Regularly Review the Network of Services

Once developed, a service-oriented approach requires continuous evaluation to foster a customer service culture. Using regular reviews of the network of services and assessment of the applied work policies, Kanban encourages the improvement of the delivered results.

Kanban Practices

When aiming to implement the Kanban method, every organization must be careful with the practical steps. Six core practices need to be present for a successful implementation. While mastering these is vital, it's an evolving process - close to 40% of all organizations admit that the way they use the Kanban practices still matures. Let's take a closer look and understand what the six practices of Kanban are.

- Visualize the workflow
- Limit work in progress
- Manage flow
- Make process policies explicit
- Implement feedback loops
- Improve collaboratively

1. Visualize the Workflow

To visualize your process with a Kanban system, you will need a board with cards and columns. Each column on the board represents a step in your workflow. Each Kanban card represents a work item. The Kanban board itself represents the actual state of your workflow with all its risks and specifications.

The first and most important thing for you is understanding what it takes to get an item from a request to a deliverable product. Recognizing how work flows through your system will set you on the path to continuous improvement by making well-observed and necessary changes.

When you start working on item X, you pull it from the "To Do" column, and when it is completed, you move it to "Done". This way, you can easily track progress and spot bottlenecks. Naturally, your Kanban board might have a different outlook as it depends on your specific needs and processes.

2. Limit Work in Progress (WIP)

One of Kanban's primary functions is to ensure a manageable number of active items are in progress at any one time. If there are no work-in-progress limits, you are not doing Kanban. Switching a team's focus halfway through will generally harm the process, and multitasking is a sure route to generating waste and inefficiency.

Limiting WIP means implementing a pull system on parts or the complete workflow. Setting maximum items per stage ensures that a card is only "pulled" into the next step when there is available capacity. Such constraints will quickly illuminate problem areas in your flow so you can identify and resolve them.

3. Manage Flow

Managing the flow is about managing the work but not the people. By flow, we mean the movement of work items through the production process at a predictable and sustainable pace.

One of the main goals when implementing a Kanban system is to create a smooth, healthy flow. Instead of micro-managing people and trying to keep them busy all the time, you should focus on managing the work processes and understanding how to get that work faster through the system. This would mean that your Kanban system is creating value more quickly.

4. Make Process Policies Explicit

You can't improve something you don't understand. Therefore, your process should be clearly defined, published, and socialized. People would not associate and participate in something they do not believe would be useful. When everyone is familiar with the common goal, they would be able to work and make decisions regarding a positive impact. Sparse, visible, well-defined, and subject to change (if/when needed), work policies have the power to boost people's self-organization.

5. Feedback Loops

For teams and companies that want to be more agile, implementing feedback loops is a mandatory step. They ensure that organizations are adequately responding to potential changes and enable knowledge transfer between stakeholders. Kanban suggests the use of cadences (feedback loops) at a team level as well as service-oriented cadences.

An example of a **team-level cadence** is the daily Team Kanban Meeting for tracking the status and the flow of work. It helps to identify available capacity and potential for increasing the delivery pace. It takes place in front of the Kanban board, and every member tells the others what they did the previous day and what they will be doing today.

Service-oriented cadences in Kanban, such as operations, service delivery, and risk meetings, aim to synchronize and improve your delivery of service. The output of these reviews, such as understanding what is blocking effective service delivery, should serve as a decision-making input for the continuous improvement of your network of services.

While focused and regular meetings with fewer attendees have proven to be a good practice, the ideal duration of specific Kanban cadences depends on your context, the team size, and topics.

6. Improve Collaboratively (Using Models & the Scientific Method)

The way to achieve continuous improvement and sustainable change within an organization is through collaboratively implementing changes based on scientifically proven methods, feedback, and metrics.

Cultivating an organizational culture where every hypothesis is proven to have positive or negative results is crucial for developing a mindset focused on improvement through evolutionary change.

Top 6 Benefits of Kanban

According to the 1st State of Kanban report, the leading reasons for adopting the Kanban method are the need for **enhanced visibility of work** and **continuous improvement**. Let's reveal some more of the benefits of using Kanban today.

- Increased visibility of the flow
- Improved delivery speed
- Alignment between goals and execution

- Improved predictability
- Improved dependencies management
- Increased customer satisfaction

Increased Visibility of the Flow

The basic idea of Kanban is visualizing every piece of work. This way, the Kanban board turns into a central informational hub, and everyone is on the same page. All tasks are visible, and they never get lost, which brings transparency to the whole work process. Every team member can have a quick update on the status of every project or task.

Improved Delivery Speed

Kanban offers multiple ways for project managers to closely monitor and make informed analyses of the distribution of work. With a clear view over the work items completed for a certain period, the stages where tasks spend the longest, bottlenecks are easy to identify. Teams are enabled to tackle these challenges to improve their workflow and, ultimately, their delivery rate.

Alignment between Business Goals and Execution

Promoting transparency, encouraging feedback, and regular review meetings, Kanban practices enable aligning the company's strategic goals with teams' day-to-day work. This alignment between the business direction and execution enhances the agility of an organization. It allows teams to adapt to changing priorities and reorganizations due to change in the market or customer's requirements.

Improved Predictability

Once you create a Kanban board and start accumulating work items on it, you'll be able to understand your process in depth with flow metrics. Analyzing the time tasks spend in your workflow (cycle time) will enable you to improve your predictions on how much work you can deliver in the future. Understanding your delivery rate consistency (throughput) will make your forecasts more accurate and your decisions based on historical data.

Improved Ability to Manage Scale and Dependencies

The intrinsic Kanban practice to visualization is also applied when it comes to mapping and managing dependencies. Starting with what you do now means visualizing the present dependencies and managing the flow between them. Managing dependencies provides both insights on the present state of a workflow and ideas for improvement. On the other hand, it also enables full transparency for strategic management over the workflow and the existing links between teams.

Increased Customer Satisfaction

The origin of the Kanban method - the pull system it is based on implies that work is done when there's a demand. In other words, Kanban navigates you to reduce waste by working solely on tasks that are needed at present. Furthermore, by applying visualization techniques and introducing work-in-progress limits to the process, you will ensure that the result is fine-tuned to your customer's expectations.

Scrum vs. Kanban

The most important difference between Kanban and Scrum is that the former is a method, while the latter is a framework. Kanban builds a continuous delivery model where teams release value as soon as they are ready, while Scrum organizes work in Sprints. Applying either one depends on the nature of your process, however, it can be said that Kanban offers a more tailor-made approach while Scrum relies on predetermined rules. Another key distinguishing characteristic between the two is the mindset and founding belief systems of Scrum and Kanban.

Kanban

Scrum

Nature

Kanban is an adaptive method

Scrum is a prescriptive framework

Principles

1. Start with what you do now
2. Agree to pursue evolutionary change
3. Encourage acts of leadership at all levels
4. Focus on customer's needs
5. Manage the work
6. Regularly review the network of services

1. Empiricism
2. Transparency
3. Inspection
4. Adaptation

Cadences

- Team-level cadences
- Service-oriented cadences

- Sprint with a fixed length
- Sprint planning
- Daily Scrum
- Sprint Review
- Sprint Retrospective

Roles

- Service Delivery Manager*
- Service Request Manager*

(*no pre-defined roles are required)

- Product Owner
- Scrum Master
- Development Team

Metrics

- Cycle Time
- Throughput
- Work In Progress
- Velocity
- Planned Capacity

What Are the Main Kanban Terms You Should Know?

At its core, Kanban is a work method that helps you optimize the flow of value through your value streams from ideation to customer. Although it looks like an easy way to improve your work processes, Kanban is more than visualizing your work. You need to pay attention to detail and get familiar with the basic Kanban terms and artifacts if you want to benefit from applying the method.

Here is a short Kanban glossary that will help you get started.

- **Kanban board:** A Kanban board is one of the Kanban method's key components and is where you visualize all work items. It should be divided into a minimum of 3 columns – Requested, In Progress, Done, representing different process stages.
- **Kanban card:** Kanban cards represent the different work items moving through a Kanban board. They contain important details about the tasks such as description, deadline, size, assignees, etc.
- **Columns:** They split the Kanban board vertically, and each of them represents a different stage of the workflow. Each Kanban board has 3 default columns: Requested, In Progress, Done. Depending on the complexity of a work process, these three stages can be divided into

many smaller sub-columns.

- **Swim lanes:** Horizontal lanes that split a Kanban board into sections. Teams use them to visually separate different work types on the same board and organize homogenous tasks together.
- **Cycle Time:** Cycle time begins at the moment when a new task enters the "in progress" stage of your workflow, and somebody is actually working on it.
- **Lead Time:** Lead time starts at the moment a new task is being requested (it doesn't matter if somebody is actually working on it) and ends with its final departure from the system.
- **Throughput:** The number of work items passing through (completed) a system or process over a certain period. The throughput is a key indicator showing how productive your team is over time.
- **Work in Progress (WIP):** This is the amount of work you are currently working on and it is not finished yet.
- **WIP limits:** Limiting work in progress means limiting the number of tasks your team can work on simultaneously to avoid overburdening and context switching.
- **Classes of Service:** Set of policies that help Agile teams prioritize work items and projects.
- **Kanban Cadences:** Cyclical meetings that drive evolutionary change and "fit for purpose" service delivery.
- **Kanban software:** Refers to a digital system that allows the practical application of the Kanban practices and principles to be used by various teams and organizations of all sizes.

Kanban in a Nutshell

A Kanban system is more than sticky notes on the wall. The easiest way to understand Kanban is to embrace its philosophy and apply it to your daily work. If you read, understand, and resonate with its core principles, the practical transition would seem logical and even inevitable.

Visualizing workflow, setting WIP limits, managing flow, ensuring explicit policies, and continuously improving will take your process far beyond what you could think. Remember to organize regular feedback loops, and all these pieces together will reveal Kanban's real power.

A3 problem solving

A3 refers to a European paper size that is roughly equivalent to an American 11-inch by 17-inch tabloid-sized paper. The A3 format is used by

Toyota as the template for three different types of reports:

- Proposals
- Status
- Problem solving

A3 problem solving is a Lean approach to reporting issues and presenting ways of addressing them. The simple method, developed by Toyota, bases on documenting a problem, together with its current outcome and a suggested change, on a single sheet of A3 paper (420x297mm), giving it the name. You can use it to make a process change proposal, report on project status, or solve a problem.

A3 takes from the Plan-Do-Check-Act cycle. Though it appears to be a step-by-step process, the method tends to be used iteratively, with the problem and solution sections being cyclically updated.

Taiichi Ōno of Toyota was known for not appreciating reports longer than one page, which helped the proliferation of the A3 approach within the automotive giant's offices. A3 is similar to the 8D report also widespread in the automotive industry, though typically for complaints management. Furthermore, the ability to quickly discern a problem and understand its solution is innate to Lean values.

Lean emphasizes visualization, with examples in value stream mapping and Kanban's visual workflows. That made a single-page report presenting what is going on was a welcome addition to a Lean operation.

Why use the A3 approach to solving problems?

Lean provides a competitive advantage, strategic and operational benefits through its objective to increase the value delivered to the customer and to reduce waste. Engaging in a process that allows the team to find the correct, best solution in the shortest possible time is highly beneficial.

Understandably, some reports and proposals must contain extensive amounts of data, and they have their place in a business environment. But imagine the value and advantage that distilling this information to 1 page has. Consider how much faster decisions can be made based on that. Besides the time savings, the opportunity to use the systematic approach of PDCA supplements the problem-solving skills required to propose accurate solutions.

It's the act of planning that is important, as it spells out all known obstacles, visualizes the action plan, and helps to foresee potential outcomes and issues along the way. While documenting your problem on an A3 piece of paper may or may not yield benefits, the act of implementing A3 thinking is what makes the difference.

The benefits of using A3 thinking are:

- Quicker problem solving through logical reasoning and application of a step-by-step, visual process. Demanding a root cause identification ensures that difficulties are dealt with, not just temporarily masked.
- Easier planning thanks to the application of objective, critical thinking promoted by the A3's structure.
- Team development through repeated use of a structural tool to find root causes of problems and their best solutions. The use of one tool across all company levels also promotes cross-department collaboration and knowledge sharing.
- Company growth A3 reports help maintain and keep company knowledge on record, helping to sustain good operating policies and build a strong growth culture rooted in solving a company's actual problems, not abstract ideas.

How to create an A3 report?

Step 1: The title

It should focus on the problem you are trying to solve and not the solution you want to convey. Examples of titles are: *"Decrease Team Misunderstanding of Task Instructions"* or *"Reduce Customer Complaints with Product XYZ"*.

Step 2: Background

According to the authors of *"Understanding A3 Thinking: A Critical Component of Toyota's PDCA Management System"*, one of the main strengths of Toyota is that they place importance on understanding a problem. Rather than rush onto a solution, Toyota takes the time to precisely understand what is going on. The principle of going on a Gemba walk attests to this need to perceive problems first-hand.

The report's background section conveys important related facts and how the problem aligns with the company's strategic objectives. Presenting this right there on the page helps minimize the cost that a board of highly paid executives would need to spend looking at a problem, without a guarantee of them understanding it, nor coming up with the right solution. Consider this checklist for your background section:

- Do I know the needs of my report's audience?
- Have I provided enough context?
- Does what it presents align with the audience's strategic goals?
- Can the background be explained in 30 seconds?

Step 3: Current condition

A correct definition and a good understanding of the problem is your path to finding the right solution. That makes working on defining the current condition 90 % of the A3 effort.

The objective here is to make sure everyone is aware of the problem, whether the report documents it appropriately, and whether anyone questions the report's findings. The use of graphs, charts, or other visual aids is beneficial.

Step 4: Goal

Your target - if you hit it, you know that your problem-solving effort has been a success. But you need to know what metrics will measure success and what the definition of success is. An example could be *"reducing customer complaints by 15%, as measured by call center statistics"*.

Step 5: The root cause

The focus of the root cause section should be to differentiate between facts and opinions regarding a problem's cause and effect. You can include your findings from 5 Whys exercises, an Ishikawa diagram, or any other result of your RCA efforts. If the root cause is not defined correctly, the problem will likely resurface, causing waste and negating the Lean principles.

Step 6: Countermeasures

The countermeasures should be the corrective actions to take for the root cause of the problem to be resolved. If not possible - without a process overhaul - you can use containment actions instead to stop the issue from directly impacting the customer. It is OK to address complex problems iteratively, along with the values of continuous improvement.

The section may include a table of the problem causes, actions taken, action owners, and the achieved results.

Step 7: Effect confirmation

Since the A3 exercise bases on the PDCA cycle, this section of your report should show the effort you expended to confirm your findings. The proof that you have indeed solved the problem. For example, software engineers include samples that replicate the bugs and verify they are no longer present after a fix.

If the exercise has not taken place yet, i.e., when you're presenting a plan to gain approval, you should outline what exercises you will conduct to check if the aim is successful.

Step 8: Follow up actions

The final section should include any other actions that you might want to consider. A principle worth adhering to here is the *"Shitsuke - sustain"* step of the 5S plan. Consider what you should do to ensure the benefits of this exercise are maintained. And could they possibly be translated to other areas of the company?

A3 Report template

Just in Time (JIT)

The just-in-time, or JIT, inventory system is a strategy in which orders of raw materials for manufacturing are aligned closely with production schedules.In a JIT system, companies keep on hand only materials that will be immediately used for the production of goods. JIT is a form of inventory management that requires working closely with suppliers so that raw materials arrive as production is scheduled to begin, but no sooner. The goal is to have the minimum amount of inventory on hand to meet demand.

The Purpose of the JIT System

The purpose of the JIT system is to reduce inventory costs by only keeping inventory of materials that are needed for products that are currently being produced. For example, Toyota, which was one of the earliest companies to adopt this strategy in 1970, may only order car parts from suppliers when they have an order for cars to be produced. This way, they avoid having to pay to store extra components, as well as preventing unused parts from degrading or depreciating.

Requirements of the JIT System

For this method to be successful, manufacturers need to be able to predict demand accurately.

The success of JIT also requires high-quality workmanship, reliable suppliers, and consistently error-free machinery. Disruptions in the supply chain can easily result in an inability to produce goods, as was the case in 1997 after a fire at a Japanese auto-parts supplier forced them to temporarily halt production. The lack of parts being supplied caused Toyota, a company that relied on them, to have to halt production for several weeks, ultimately costing them over $1 billion in revenue.

How Does Just-in-Time Inventory Management Work?

JIT inventory management ensures that stock arrives as it is needed for production or to meet consumer demand, but no sooner. The goal is to eliminate waste and increase the efficiency of your operations. Since the main objective is often quality and not the lowest price, JIT requires long-term contracts with reliable suppliers.

JIT is what's known as a lean management process. In JIT, all parts of any production or service system, particularly people, are interconnected. They inform each other and are mutually dependent on generating successful outcomes. This practice's origin comes from Kaizen, a Japanese term meaning "change for the better." Originating in Japan, the business philosophy looks to continuously improve operations and involve all employees, from assembly line workers to the CEO. Like JIT, the goal is to reduce waste and improve quality.

Organizations may vary in how they implement JIT in their environment, but the general steps are the same. This diagram shows how the cycle of continuous improvement works in JIT inventory management.

Steps in Cycle of Continuous Improvement for JIT Inventory

1. **Design:** The JIT process begins with a review of the essential manufacturing building blocks: product design, process design, personnel and manufacturing planning. Then plans are put into place to eliminate disruption, minimize waste and build a flexible system.
2. **Manage:** A *Total Quality Management (TQM)* review ensures there is continuous improvement throughout the process. A management review defines workers' roles and responsibilities, defines and measures statistical quality control, stabilizes schedules, and checks out load and capacity schedules and levels.
3. **Pull:** Educate the team on production and withdrawal methods using signaling methods like Kanban. Review lot size policies and reduce lot sizes.
4. **Establish:** Vendor relationships are vital to the success of JIT. Review vendor lists. Settle on preferred suppliers, negotiate contracts, discuss lead times, delivery expectations and usage metrics and measures. Learn how to make the most of them in the supply chain.
5. **Fine-tune:** Determine inventory needs, policies, controls and reduce inventory movements.
6. **Build:** Inform your team about the skills and capabilities it needs to complete its work and conduct team education and empowerment sessions to educate them.
7. **Refine:** Reduce the number of parts and steps in production by refining, standardizing and reviewing the entire process.
8. **Review:** Define and implement quality measures and metrics and conduct a root cause analysis of any problems. Emphasize improvements and track trends to improve every aspect of JIT.

Advantages of JIT Inventory Management

JIT inventory management boosts a company's ROI by lowering inventory carrying costs, increasing efficiency and decreasing waste.

- **Waste Reduction:** The JIT inventory management model eliminates overordering and excess of all kinds.
  - **Reduce Obsolete Inventory and Dead Stock:** Low inventory levels significantly reduce the risk of inventory going unsold and sitting in

the warehouse obsolete.

- **Reduce Defective Product Loss:** Defective inventory items are easier to identify and fix when production levels are low, which reduces scrap costs.

- **Improved Efficiency:** JIT eliminates the costs that come with extra raw materials, unneeded inventory and product storage.

  - **Raise Inventory Turnover Ratios:** Greater efficiency brings higher inventory turnover.
  - **Minimal Inventory Obsolescence:** The high inventory turnover rate keeps items from sitting in your facility for too long and becoming obsolete.
  - **Minimize Raw Materials on Hand:** Receiving deliveries in the smallest possible quantities—sometimes multiple times per day—virtually eliminates raw material inventories.
  - **Local Sourcing:** When suppliers are located near a company's production facility, the shortened distances contribute to timely deliveries. On-time, reliable delivery of goods reduces the need for safety stock.

- **Greater Productivity:** JIT enhances productivity by reducing the time and resources involved in manufacturing processes.

  - **Faster Product Turnaround:** Manufacturers can more quickly produce products.
  - **Shorter Production Runs:** With JIT, manufacturers can deliver new products more quickly and easily.
  - **Simplify Change Orders:** Having less raw material stock to draw down before product changes makes it easier to implement engineering change orders to existing products.

- **Smoother Production Flow:** JIT can eliminate bottlenecks and delays across the entire production process.

  - **Shorter Production Cycles:** JIT shortens manufacturing time, which decreases lead times for customers.

- **Reduce Product Defects:** Production mistakes can be spotted faster and corrected, which results in fewer defective products.
- **Shorter Production Runs:** Fast equipment setup times reduce production runs, lowering investment in finished goods.
- **More Functional Production Cells:** Employees walk individual parts through the processing steps in a work cell, which reduces scrap levels. Cell models also eliminate work-in-process queues that build up at more specialized workstations.
- **Compressed Operations:** Arranging production work cells near each other limits the amount of work-in-process inventory moving between cells.

▪ **Lower Costs:** Receiving goods on an as-needed basis reduces inventory costs.

- **Reduce Working Capital:** The low inventory levels that come with JIT limit the amount of working capital needed.
- **Lower Holding Costs:** Inventory holding costs (like those for warehousing) are minimal because less space is used.
- **Lower Cash Investment:** Companies invest less cash in inventory because JIT doesn't require having a lot of stock on hand.
- **Reduce Large Raw Material Spends:** In JIT, businesses order raw material when needed, so cash is available for other uses that could be more valuable to the company.
- **Reduce Labor Costs:** Labor expenses are lower since the number of person-hours required to fulfill orders is usually fewer than full-time production.

▪ **Improve Quality:** A flexible workforce can focus on making quality products with lower defect rates. Better outcomes increase customer satisfaction and reduce the cash outlay for production.

- **Reduce Work-in-Progress Goods:** Fewer items moving on the shop floor allows teams to focus on building high-quality products.
- **Less Damage:** Since minimal inventory is on hand, storage-related accidents decline.
- **Certified Quality:** Suppliers guarantee quality in advance. So, deliveries go straight to production areas instead of being held in

receiving to await inspection.

To support these goals, you can invest in new technology or update existing solutions that will link your system with your suppliers to coordinate the delivery of parts and materials.

JIT Inventory Methodology

The JIT inventory methodology uses a variety of techniques to smooth operations. The lean method focuses on optimizing organization, paying attention to detail, having small lot sizes, increasing transparency, fostering cell manufacturing and using a pull (rather than push) approach.

Techniques Involved in JIT Inventory Methodology

- **Order:** Maintain a high level of physical and organizational discipline.
- **Better Quality:** Eliminate defects through attention to detail and continuous improvements.
- **Reduced Setup Time:** Create flexible changeover approaches when setups need to adjust to meet customer demand.
- **Small Lot Size:** In JIT, one is the ideal lot size. The small size reduces in-process inventory, carrying costs, storage space, and makes for easier inspection and rework.
- **Load Uniformity:** Leveling is a control mechanism that achieves a stable, level daily schedule.
- **Flow Balance:** Flow scheduling organizes throughput for even distribution of energy and labor.
- **Diversified Skills:** Cross-trained workers can be deployed to different areas to keep production moving.
- **Visibility for Control:** Using communication tools, like those found in Kanban, keeps the entire team informed of inventory levels.
- **Ongoing Maintenance:** Ongoing oversight and focus on detail, including the machinery and tools the business uses every day, helps maintain a low defect, low problem environment.
- **Use Fitness:** JIT spaces designed to fit each process speeds up production. One workstation pulls output from the one before it, as needed, based on a master schedule or customer demand.
- **Logical Plant Layout:** Product-oriented design makes assembly easier and more efficient.
- **Strong Supplier Network:** Strong relationships with vendors make JIT inventory most effective.

- **Worker Immersion:** Every team member should be dedicated to the process and colleagues to achieve JIT goals.
- **Cell Manufacturing:** Create an environment where groups can work as quickly as possible to make as many products as they can and limit the waste they create.
- **Pull System:** The process of only replacing products once they've been used in production.

Disadvantages of Just-in-Time Inventory Techniques

JIT inventory management relies heavily on precise forecasting and strong relationships with key suppliers. When something goes wrong with either of those, that's a problem because there are no backup options in place. For example, a single supplier that can't deliver for any period of time can disrupt the entire supply chain and halt your operations. In addition, companies practicing strict JIT inventory management probably won't have extra stock to satisfy unexpected orders.

If an organization's forecasting can't account for a surge in demand, for instance, it won't have the stock to fill those orders. That could mean lost revenue and, potentially, lost customers.

Potential Risks of Just-in-Time Inventory

The primary risk of JIT comes from its philosophy. JIT inventory management requires everyone in an ecosystem and supply chain to commit and work cohesively. If any part of that arrangement breaks down, it risks the entire infrastructure.

- **Lack of Preparedness:** The business's entire workflow needs to convert to a lean framework. These actions affect the organization and the supply chain, which may need to change its procedures and practices.
- **Supply Chain Disruptions:** Disruptions in the supply chain can stall the production process.
- **Missed Opportunities:** With few or no finished goods on hand, a company may not be able to meet massive and unexpected orders immediately.
- **Unexpected Price Changes:** In JIT, the cost for parts is constant. When costs rise, profit margins drop.
- **Overreliance on Forecasts:** Adapting to sudden surges or declines is difficult because of the reliance on forecasting.
- **Order Issues:** Shortages and stock-outs can disrupt inventory systems.

- **Local Sourcing Costs:** JIT relies on local sourcing, which can cost more for a number of different reasons. This dependency can also affect profitability in the pursuit of reliability.
- **Time Pressure:** Scheduling may increase the cost of goods sold (COGS) because there's no guarantee a company will always have the best price for raw materials from a supplier.
- **Undisciplined Staff:** Team members that are not on board with JIT can affect productivity, quality and other issues.
- **Supplier Dependence:** A supplier who does not deliver goods on time and in the right amounts can disrupt the entire production process.
- **Acts of Nature:** A natural disaster that interferes with a vendor's flow of goods can halt production.

Questions

1. What is a lean system?
2. What are the guiding principles of a lean system?
3. What are the features of lean in manufacturing and services?
4. Describe Lean management concepts?
5. Explain the process of value stream mapping?
6. What is continuous improvement?
7. Explain the procedure for a workflow analysis?
8. Explain the procedure for creating a workflow?
9. Create a workflow diagram of Swiggy delivery?
10. Explain about lot size? How many types of lot sizes are there?
11. Explain the differences between pull and push system?
12. What is Kanban? Explain the principles of Kanban?
13. How is Kanban implemented in workplaces?
14. Describe about A3 problem solving?
15. What is JIT? Explain the advantages and disadvantages of JIT?

References

1. Costa, J. M., Rossi, M., Rebentisch, E., Terzi, S., Taisch, M., & Nightingale, D. (2014). What to measure for success in lean system engineering programs?. *Procedia Computer Science, 28*, 789-798.
2. Liker, J. K. (1997). *Becoming lean: Inside stories of US manufacturers.* CRC Press.

3. Taylor, A., Taylor, M., & McSweeney, A. (2013). Towards greater understanding of success and survival of lean systems. *International Journal of Production Research, 51*(22), 6607-6630.
4. Paez, O., Dewees, J., Genaidy, A., Tuncel, S., Karwowski, W., & Zurada, J. (2004). The lean manufacturing enterprise: An emerging sociotechnological system integration. *Human Factors and Ergonomics in Manufacturing & Service Industries, 14*(3), 285-306.
5. Lyonnet, B., & Toscano, R. (2014). Towards an adapted lean system–a push-pull manufacturing strategy. *Production Planning & Control, 25*(4), 346-354.
6. Keyser, R. S., & Sawhney, R. S. (2013). Reliability in lean systems. *International Journal of Quality & Reliability Management.*
7. Moayed, F. A., & Shell, R. L. (2009). Comparison and evaluation of maintenance operations in lean versus non-lean production systems. *Journal of Quality in Maintenance Engineering.*
8. Hines, P., & Rich, N. (1997). The seven value stream mapping tools. *International journal of operations & production management.*
9. Singh, B., Garg, S. K., & Sharma, S. K. (2011). Value stream mapping: literature review and implications for Indian industry. *The International Journal of Advanced Manufacturing Technology, 53*(5), 799-809.
10. Rother, M., & Shook, J. (2003). *Learning to see: value stream mapping to add value and eliminate muda.* Lean Enterprise Institute.
11. van Der Aalst, W. M., Ter Hofstede, A. H., Kiepuszewski, B., & Barros, A. P. (2003). Workflow patterns. *Distributed and parallel databases, 14*(1), 5-51.
12. Georgakopoulos, D., Hornick, M., & Sheth, A. (1995). An overview of workflow management: From process modeling to workflow automation infrastructure. *Distributed and parallel Databases, 3*(2), 119-153.
13. Van Der Aalst, W., Van Hee, K. M., & van Hee, K. (2004). *Workflow management: models, methods, and systems.* MIT press.
14. Junior, M. L., & Godinho Filho, M. (2010). Variations of the kanban system: Literature review and classification. *International Journal of Production Economics, 125*(1), 13-21.
15. Akturk, M. S., & Erhun, F. (1999). An overview of design and operational issues of kanban systems. *International Journal of Production Research, 37*(17), 3859-3881.

16. Sendil Kumar, C., & Panneerselvam, R. (2007). Literature review of JIT-KANBAN system. *The International Journal of Advanced Manufacturing Technology*, *32*(3), 393-408.
17. Rahman, N. A. A., Sharif, S. M., & Esa, M. M. (2013). Lean manufacturing case study with Kanban system implementation. *Procedia Economics and Finance*, *7*, 174-180.
18. Ahmad, M. O., Markkula, J., & Oivo, M. (2013, September). Kanban in software development: A systematic literature review. In *2013 39th Euromicro conference on software engineering and advanced applications* (pp. 9-16). IEEE.
19. Sobek II, D. K., & Jimmerson, C. (2004). A3 reports: tool for process improvement. In *IIE Annual Conference. Proceedings* (p. 1). Institute of Industrial and Systems Engineers (IISE).
20. Matthews, D. D. (2018). *The A3 workbook: Unlock your problem-solving mind*. CRC Press.
21. Flinchbaugh, J. (2012). A3 problem solving: Applying lean thinking. *Lean Learning Center*, 533-538.
22. Saad, N. M., Al-Ashaab, A., Shehab, E., & Maksimovic, M. (2013). A3 thinking approach to support problem solving in lean product and process development. In *Concurrent Engineering Approaches for Sustainable Product Development in a Multi-Disciplinary Environment* (pp. 871-882). Springer, London.
23. Sobek II, D. K., & Jimmerson, C. (2006). A3 reports: Tool for organizational transformation. In *IIE annual conference. Proceedings* (p. 1). Institute of Industrial and Systems Engineers (IISE).
24. Fullerton, R. R., & McWatters, C. S. (2001). The production performance benefits from JIT implementation. *Journal of operations management*, *19*(1), 81-96.

CHAPTER IV

Project Selection for Lean

Project Selection for Lean

- Resource and project selection,
- Selecting projects,
- Process mapping,
- Current and future value stream mapping,

Project selection is one of the key success factors for the launch phase. As a change agent driving Lean transformation, it's not enough to just have the technical skills. A change agent must also be fully aware of what nurtures and derails a Lean transformation. For one, change agents must know that a successful Lean transformation requires the right context. Many times, such Lean initiatives fail because ill-selected projects do not end up producing the desired business results.

The project selection process is started in the Executive workshop where areas for improvement are identified. Initial projects are selected in the Champion workshop based on the improvement areas identified by the executives, project selection criteria, and the project chartering process.

Selecting Appropriate Projects for Lean Improvement.

A project is particularly suitable for Lean improvement if it meets at least one of the following requirements:

- Targets end-to-end processes that will impact strategic business objectives and outcomes
- Targets processes mired in complexity and needing simplification
- Targets processes associated with customer issues and complaints
- Targets high-cost processes that consume more resources than required
- Targets business units where there are problems around manpower productivity
- Enhances core-competencies for the business
- Helps in improving the top line/bottom-line of the business

- Improves the competitive position of the business
- Helps to install processes and process thinking

Projects to Avoid for Lean Improvement

A project is not suitable for Lean improvement if it has any one of the following:

- Targets a business undergoing major change
- Targets a process that is undergoing a transition
- Will not impact key business objectives and results
- Targets a process that is broken and not end-to-end
- Does not have a senior leader willing to sponsor it
- Will compete with many other change initiatives for resources
- Does not have an assured guarantee that its Sponsor/business leader will spend time reviewing its progress
- Does not have an assured guarantee that its process teams will invest the time in the project
- Will have a Sponsor who will maintain a hands-off approach during its deployment
- Will only be completed to manage internal politics or settle internal scores
- Already has a known solution
- Has a problem that is too big
- Is expected to produce vague results

Project selection is a critical part of the Six Sigma quality improvement process. Just like other Six Sigma tools, project selection is quantifiable and based on objective data rather than subjective guesswork.

A project is a problem that is scheduled for solution. A good Six Sigma project is connected to a company's strategic goals and will solve customers' problems. A successful project will lead to improvements in schedule, quality or cost and can be used to meet the needs of external customers, internal customers or shareholders. Because an organization only has so many Black Belts and Green Belts, only the projects with the greatest benefit to the company and the greatest probability for success are implemented.

The rigors of Six Sigma require that project selection be based on quantifiable metrics. Choosing a project based on quantifiable data helps the organization identify the project that provides the greatest savings relative to the time expended and cost of deployment.

Pareto priority index

A cost-benefit analysis can be performed on the potential project to determine its estimated benefit to the organization. This analysis is known as the Pareto priority index (PPI). The index takes account of the following elements:

Savings – This a dollar amount, determined by the accounting department, that reflects savings that result from increased sales, decreased labor costs, decreased carrying costs, and reduced maintenance and material costs.

Probability of success – Not all projects will be successful. This figure is expressed as a percentage and indicates how likely the project is to achieve its stated goal.

Cost – This dollar amount, determined by the accounting department, illustrates the price of implementing a project. This figure includes costs such as materials, work stoppage for data collection and labor costs.

Completion time – This is the time required for the project team to complete the DMAIC process and implement the solution.

The PPI weighs the dollar savings and the probability of success of a project against the cost of deployment and the time required for project completion. The result is illustrated in an index number.

The index number helps organizations compare a several different potential projects at a glance. Potential projects with greater dollar savings and a higher probability of success will have a higher PPI number than those with greater cost and longer completion time.

Prioritization Matrix

While the cost-benefit analysis of the Pareto prioritization index has the advantages of being based on objective and quantitative factors that provide a metric that is useful for comparing different projects, it lacks the benefit of customer input. Because the best projects are those that solve a customer's problem, the PPI must be balanced with a prioritization matrix that captures the customer's needs.

The project selection committee draws upon customer surveys, interviews and focus groups to gain the voice of the customer. The potential project recommendations provided by customers are then placed into a matrix where every potential project is compared to every other potential project. The project selection committee then rates each project and the one with the greatest benefit to the company is chosen.

When Six Sigma projects are selected based the quantitative rigor of the Pareto Priority Index and a prioritization matrix that displays customer needs, it helps to ensure that the Six Sigma project benefits both to the company and the customer.

What is Process Mapping

A process map is a planning and management tool that visually describes the flow of work. Using process mapping software, process maps show a series of events that produce an end result. A process map is also called a flowchart, process flowchart, process chart, functional process chart, functional flowchart, process model, workflow diagram, business flow diagram or process flow diagram. It shows who and what is involved in a process and can be used in any business or organization and can reveal areas where a process should be improved.

Purpose of process mapping

The purpose of process mapping is for organizations and businesses to improve efficiency. Process maps provide insight into a process, help teams brainstorm ideas for process improvement, increase communication and provide process documentation. Process mapping will identify bottlenecks, repetition and delays. They help to define process boundaries, process ownership, process responsibilities and effectiveness measures or process metrics.

Understanding processes

One of the purposes of process mapping is to gain better understanding of a process. The flowchart below is a good example of using process mapping to understand and improve a process. In this chart, the process is making pasta. Even though this is a very simplified process map example, many parts of business use similar diagrams to understand processes and improve process efficiency, such as operations, finance, supply chain, sales, marketing and accounting.

Benefits of process mapping

Process mapping spotlights waste, streamlines work processes and builds understanding. Process mapping allows you to visually communicate the important details of a process rather than writing extensive directions.

Flowcharts and process maps are used to:

- Increase understanding of a process
- Analyze how a process could be improved
- Show others how a process is done
- Improve communication between individuals engaged in the same process
- Provide process documentation
- Plan projects

Process maps can save time and simplify projects because they:

- Create and speed up the project design
- Provide effective visual communication of ideas, information and data
- Help with problem solving and decision making
- Identify problems and possible solutions
- Can be built quickly and economically
- Show processes broken down into steps and use symbols that are easy to follow
- Show detailed connections and sequences
- Show an entire process from the beginning to the end

Process maps help you to understand the important characteristics of a process, allowing you to produce helpful data to use in problem solving. Process maps let you strategically ask important questions that help you improve any process.

Types of process mapping

Process mapping is about communicating your process to others. You can build stronger understanding with process maps. The most common process map types include:

- **Activity Process Map**: represents value added and non-value-added activities in a process
- **Detailed Process Map**: provides a much more detailed look at each step in the process
- **Document Map**: documents are the inputs and outputs in a process
- **High-Level Process Map**: high-level representation of a process involving interactions between Supplier, Input, Process, Output, Customer (SIPOC)

- **Rendered Process Map**: represents current state and/or future state processes to show areas for process improvement
- **Swimlane (or Cross-functional) Map**: separates out the sub-process responsibilities in the process
- **Value-Added Chain Diagram**: unconnected boxes that represent a very simplified version of a process for quick understanding
- **Value Stream Map**: a lean-management technique that analyzes and improves processes needed to make a product or provide a service to a customer.
- **Work Flow Diagram**: a work process shown in "flow" format; doesn't utilize Unified Modeling Language (UML) symbols.

Process mapping symbols

Key elements of process mapping include actions, activity steps, decision points, functions, inputs/outputs, people involved, process measurements and time required. Basic symbols are used in a process map to describe key process elements. Each process element is represented by a specific symbol such as an arrow, circle, diamond, box, oval or rectangle.

Shape

Name

Use

Activity/ Process

Activity/Process

To represent a step/ activity of a process

Decision

Decision

To represent a decision that has to be made

Start or End

Start/ End

To represent the start and end of a process

Arrow

Arrow

To represent the connection between two steps and the direction of flow

Document

Document

To represent data or information that can be read by people

Process Map Symbols

Each step in a process is represented by a shape in a process map. These shapes are also called flowchart shapes.

There are nearly 30 standard shapes that you *can* use in process mapping. However, we think for most people, using a handful of the most common shapes will be easier to understand.

Business process mapping

In business, a process is a group of interrelated tasks that happen as a result of an event. These tasks produce a desired result for the customer. Process mapping can be used in many areas of business: business process improvement, business process redesign, reengineering, training, quality improvement, simulation, information technology, work measurement, documentation, process analysis, operational process design, process integration, acquisitions, mergers and selling business operations. Business process mapping can also be helpful for complying with manufacturing and service industry regulations, such as the common **ISO 9000(International Organization for Standardization)** or **ISO 9001**.

How to create a process map

Process mapping has become streamlined because of software that provides a better understanding of processes. Process maps can be created in common programs like Microsoft Word, PowerPoint or Excel, but there are other programs more customized to creating a process map. Process mapping is about communicating your process to others so that you achieve your management objectives. Knowing how to map a process will help you build stronger communication and understanding in your organization.

Step 1: Identify the problem

- What is the process that needs to be visualized?
- Type its title at the top of the document.

Step 2: Brainstorm activities involved

- At this point, sequencing the steps isn't important, but it may help you to remember the steps needed for your process.
- Decide what level of detail to include.
- Determine who does what and when it is done.

Step 3: Figure out boundaries

- Where or when does the process start?
- Where or when does the process stop?

Step 4: Determine and sequence the steps

- It's helpful to have a verb begin the description.
- You can show either the general flow or every detailed action or decision.

Step 5: Draw basic flowchart symbols

Each element in a process map is represented by a specific flowchart symbol. Lucid chart makes it simple to create and rearrange shapes, add labels and comments and even use custom styling in your process map.

- Ovals show the beginning of a process or the stopping of a process.
- Rectangles show an operation or activity that needs to be done.
- Arrows represent the flow of direction.
- Diamonds show a point where a decision must be made. Arrows coming out of a diamond are usually labeled yes or no. Only one arrow comes out of an activity box. If more than is needed, you should probably use a decision diamond.

- A parallelogram shows inputs or outputs.

Step 6: Finalize the process flowchart

- Review the flowchart with others stakeholders (team member, workers, supervisors, suppliers, customers, etc.) for consensus.
- Make sure you've included important chart information like a title and date, which will make it easy to reference.
- Helpful questions to ask:
    - Is the process being run how it should?
    - Will team members follow the charted process?
    - Is everyone in agreement with the process map flow?
    - Is anything redundant?
    - Are any steps missing?

Process maps provide valuable insights into how a business or an organization can improve processes. When important information is presented visually, it increases understanding and collaboration for any project.

Value stream mapping (VSM)

Value stream mapping (VSM) is defined as a lean tool that employs a flowchart documenting every step in the process. Many lean practitioners see VSM as a fundamental tool to identify waste, reduce process cycle times, and implement process improvement. VSM is a workplace efficiency tool designed to combine material processing steps with information flow, along with other important related data. VSM is an essential lean tool for an organization wanting to plan, implement, and improve while on its lean journey. VSM helps users create a solid implementation plan that will maximize their available resources and help ensure that materials and time are used efficiently.

The original VSM template was created by Toyota Motor Company and implemented via material and process flowcharts. This VSM illustrated the necessary process steps that existed from order entry to final product delivery and was useful for gaining a wide-reaching view of the company's activities. It allowed Toyota to remove nonessential activities that created waste while maintaining the manufacturing process.

The "value stream" portion of the VSM system centers on how value can be added to a product or service by changing the market form or function to meet the customer's needs. This includes adding features and functionality to a product or service that benefit the customer without increasing wasted time and materials (also called *muda*, the Japanese term for waste) on the company's side. Value Stream Mapping (VSM) is a tool to support planning and executing performance improvement in your organization, and is split into two views – current and future state maps.

The two are not mutually exclusive.

In fact, while a current state VSM is worthwhile to gauge your existing processes, it is only by setting out the desired state (the futured / ideal state) that you can know where you aim to be and ensure your process improvements are fruitful.

The current state maps

The current state VSM identifies the existing process flow, and allows your team to analyse the related data to identify gaps in process and / or wastage which can be streamlined for efficiencies.

Value Stream Mapping provides you with a single current state map that acts as an incredibly effective way of managing cross-functional problem solving:

- You can highlight areas of customer and internal pain on a single wall, all visible at the same time
- You can build out problem statements and the findings of your root cause analysis in a powerful visual way (hint – look upstream)
- Specific points where you know an improvement needs to be scoped and defined in detail can be added to the relevant points in the current state map (these are often referred to as Kaizen bursts)
- Stakeholders love Value Stream Maps – as the picture starts to build you may find an increasing number of 'visitors' of increasing importance in the organization popping their head into the room interested in a quick overview.

So there you have it – on a single wall you have a way of facilitating a large complex, cross-functional group through your traditional improvement process, but in a way that continually reinforces the performance goals of the value stream in relation to customer expectation, flow, and cross-functional efficiency.

Your improvements will often focus on activity within an upstream function for down-stream benefit, attacking the wait time or inventory between process steps or the 'hand-shake' points where different functions are handing work off to each other.

From a services perspective, a key source of improvement will not necessarily be to re-engineer how each process step is done.

The focus is more on the gaps in between process steps as above but biased towards how the most steps can be completed in the minimum number of customer contacts.

Regardless of your industry, you can see that Value Stream Mapping as a tool can help you frame and manage a traditional improvement cycle at a much greater cross-functional scale.

The future state maps

The future state VSM examines the ideal of how your process should look and work.

This is your opportunity to shortcut the improvement cycle and get straight to exciting, creative, disruptive solution mode. The goal here is to produce a view of what the future state could be and rely on improvements being defined through the observable gaps between the current and future state.

Beyond ensuring you retain a balanced view to the components of your map (customer, supplier, value delivery and monitoring and control) there is very little prescribed structure to follow here.

Some advice on future state maps

Here are some pointers of advice from my experience that, while not specific to Value Stream Mapping, are relevant to any challenge to deliver a future state:

1) Consider time in your workshop agenda for ensuring that attendees move from Current State to a creative Future state mindset.

2) Consider the reality of the influence that you have over this improvement versus the frame of reference of your workshop attendees.

a) What is your future state 1?

- Can be delivered with minimal capital investment, a focus purely on people, process, and light technology change
- A timeline of 6 months

b) What is your future state 2?

- No constraints on budget or investment required
- A multi-year timeline of delivery

3) If you are limited in creative thought on how to transform rather than incrementally improve parts of your business, consider the acronym of SECAR:

- Simplify – can you process improve, take out the waste?
- Eliminate – can you eliminate the need for the process in the first place?
- Consolidate – can you merge some processes or the capacity that is delivering that?
- Automate – can technology support your delivery?
- Reallocate – should somebody else (e.g. upstream) be doing this work?

Scoping Out Your Value Stream Map

Understanding the scope of the value stream under examination is a good start when planning your lean process or value stream map. This map is a single area in your organization. However, when multiple plants, customers, or suppliers are included, an extended level map is created.

Consider an extended level map as the view of the values stream at 60,000 feet, the facility level map at 30,000 feet, and the process level map at 10,000 feet. It is best to start at diagramming a facility level map before attempting to draw a process level map or extended level map so you do not optimize one area and suboptimize another.

Step 1: Form a Team to Create the Lean Value Stream Map

Form a cross-functional team of high-level managers and supervisors from throughout your company. Representatives from multiple departments, such as sales, customer service, inventory, operations, and beyond, will help ensure that information can be passed freely back and forth, and that items don't slip through the cracks. Consider also adding important suppliers to this group because an outside perspective can be helpful.

- The ideal team size is about 10 members. Small teams can miss important items, while large teams can end up being difficult to manage and coordinate.

Step 2: The Kaizen Kick-Off – VSM Planning

After you've formed your VSM team, your next step is to hold a three-day kaizen event (see Table 1). *Kaizen* is Japanese and means "change for the better." During a kaizen, team members begin developing current and future plans.

At the kaizen event, the team must complete four important steps:

1. Determine the process family.
2. Draw the current state map.
3. Determine and draw the future state map.
4. Draft a plan to arrive at the future state.

Once these four steps have been completed and the team agrees with the plans and tactics, the VSM team can proceed to the next steps.

Step 3: The Process Family – VSM Planning

A process family, also known as a product family, is a group of products or services that go through the same or similar processing steps. To determine your process family, create a matrix similar to the example shown in Figure 1 below.

Process Family Matrix Example

Value Stream Mapping, The Process Family Matrix

Along the top row, write all the process steps your organization performs from a 30,000-foot point of view.

- In the first column, write down the parts (e.g., components, stock keeping units, finished good items, or services) your organization makes or provides.
- Place an X in the corresponding box if the part goes through the processing step.

It's important that this step is applied to all cross-functional teams and key areas within your company. This helps ensure all vital steps are included and no steps are overlooked.\

Step 4: Identifying Similarities

Examine the matrix and look for sections that have similar or identical processing steps. Also look for sections that share about 80% of the steps.

Consider items that share many of the same steps and procedures that can be created together—by the same workers using similar or related steps—more efficiently in a manufacturing cell.

Once you've identified similarities, the team must then identify which process family it will concentrate on first. The list below represents some common reasons for picking certain areas, and they are areas that the VSM team should consider:

- Biggest "bang for the buck"
- Largest reduction in lead time or inventory
- Biggest impact to the customer
- Highest probability for success
- Most visible to stakeholders
- New product or service line
- Volume or quantity

Step 5: Creating the Current State Map – VSM Planning

To create a current state map, collect the data and information by "walking the flow" and interviewing the people who perform the task. This is beneficial for two reasons:

1. The team will have the opportunity to see the entire process and look for waste.
2. The people who actually perform the work (e.g., operators, assemblers, technicians) can answer questions and clarify any misconceptions or preconceived notions on how tasks are performed.

When your team is "walking the flow," be sure to gather high-value information from employees, including:

- Cycle time or processing time
- Changeover time
- Reliability of equipment
- First pass yield
- Quantities
- Number of operators and shifts
- Hard copy information
- Electronic information

- Inventory levels
- Queue or waiting times

The information gathered does not have to be perfect or overly detailed. As long as the data provides a relatively clear picture of major issues, the team can begin building its lean process map.

Step 6: Start by Creating the Basic VSM Template

Once your team has gathered and reviewed the information obtained while "walking the flow," begin drawing the value stream map. Figure 2 below shows some common examples and strategies with VSM template development.

Common VSM Icons

Value Stream Mapping Template Development

Key areas on the map are:

- The upper-right corner for customer information

- The upper-left corner for supplier information
- The top half of the paper for information flow
- The bottom half for material (or product) flow
- The gutters on top and bottom to calculate value added and nonvalue added time

Calculate the cycle time vs. the inventory time (in days) for the material and information flow. Each VSM will look slightly different depending on the process and how it was drawn. Figure 3 below features an example of a VSM current state map used for a metal fabricating company.

VSM Current State Map Example

Value Stream Mapping Current State Map Example

If this is one of the team's first VSM kaizens, have the facilitator draw the map on a large dry-erase board and then have the team members draw each of their own maps on paper (ideally in pencil). The current state map is usually completed by the second day, but it may need refining.

Step 7: Creating the Future State Map

- **What is the takt time?**
    - *Takt* is the German word for the baton a conductor uses to control his orchestra's speed, beat, and timing. Takt time refers to how frequently a part or component must be produced to meet your customers' demand. The formula is the time available (per shift) divided by the demand (per shift). For example:
        - 22,000 seconds (time available)
        - ÷ 200 pieces (demand)
        - = 110 seconds/piece
- **Are there bottlenecks or constraints?**
    - From the data collection during the kaizen, look at the cycle times or processing times. If any of these are greater than your takt time, you have a candidate for a bottleneck or constraint. This may be causing overproduction waste or work in process (WIP) in some areas, or extra processing time, such as overtime, to meet demand.
- **Where can inventory (or queue time) be reduced or supermarkets used?**
    - A supermarket is a controlled inventory system—the downstream process removes items from the shelf and the process owners upstream replenish that amount to the supermarket.
    - Look at raw material, WIP, buffer stock, safety stock, and finished goods inventories to see whether these can be reduced. Does it make sense to put in a supermarket replenishment system?
    - The key is to find ways to reduce inventory in a logical manner. Also look for opportunities for paperwork to flow and not sit around, like in batching.
- **Where can you improve flow?**
    - Is it possible to put materials into a cell or eliminate materials from stopping and waiting? If flow improvement isn't possible, could a "first in, first out" lane be established between processes?

- **What other improvements are required?**
  - For instance, does the reliability of equipment need to be improved? Are the first pass yield or quality levels acceptable? Is training in 5S (workplace organization) needed? Does a new layout for an area need to be created?

On the VSM, place a kaizen burst (a sticky note or thought bubble) around any items to signal improvement is needed. Items may include low equipment reliability or first pass yield; long changeover times; large batches; any waste such as overproduction, motion, transportation, waiting, defects, or adjustments; and over or extra processing.

Step 8: Creating the VSM Draft Plan

During a typical VSM event, it is possible to create the draft plan based on the information from the future state map. The plan will need further refinement, especially in determining resources required, such as time, people, and budgets. A good plan, as shown in the example below, will include the description of the project, name of the project leader, possible team members, a schedule (or Gantt chart) of events and deliverables, an estimate of costs, and the impact, goals, or benefits.

Questions

1. What is a project and explain the process of selecting an appropriate project for lean?
2. What are the projects to be avoided for lean implementation?
3. Explain about pareto priority index?
4. Describe the process of using prioritization matrix?
5. What is process mapping? Explain the need for process mapping?
6. Explain the process of creating a process map with a diagram?
7. How to create a past and future value stream mapping?

References

1. Singh, M., Rathi, R., Antony, J., & Garza-Reyes, J. A. (2021). Lean six sigma project selection in a manufacturing environment using hybrid methodology based on intuitionistic fuzzy MADM approach. *IEEE Transactions on Engineering Management*.

2. Kornfeld, B., & Kara, S. (2013). Selection of Lean and Six Sigma projects in industry. *International Journal of Lean Six Sigma.*
3. Shukla, V., Swarnakar, V., & Singh, A. R. (2021). Prioritization of lean six sigma project selection criteria using best worst method. *Materials Today: Proceedings, 47,* 5749-5754.
4. Ray, S., & Das, P. (2010). Six Sigma project selection methodology. *International Journal of Lean Six Sigma.*
5. Padhy, R. K., & Sahu, S. (2011). A Real Option based Six Sigma project evaluation and selection model. *International Journal of Project Management, 29*(8), 1091-1102.
6. Damelio, R. (2011). *The basics of process mapping.* CRC press.
7. Hunt, V. D. (1996). *Process mapping: how to reengineer your business processes.* John Wiley & Sons.
8. Klotz, L., Horman, M., Bi, H. H., & Bechtel, J. (2008). The impact of process mapping on transparency. *International Journal of Productivity and Performance Management.*
9. Soliman, F. (1998). Optimum level of process mapping and least cost business process re-engineering. *International Journal of Operations & Production Management.*
10. Aldowaisan, T. A., & Gaafar, L. K. (1999). Business process reengineering: an approach for process mapping. *Omega, 27*(5), 515-524.
11. Madison, D. (2005). *Process mapping, process improvement, and process management: a practical guide for enhancing work and information flow.* Paton Professional.
12. Fiore, S. M., & Schooler, J. W. (2004). Process mapping and shared cognition: Teamwork and the development of shared problem models.

CHAPTER V

Lean Management and Implementation

Lean Management and Implementation

- Standardized work
- continuous improvement.
- Lean projects: Training, selecting the members, preparing project plan, implementation, review.
- Productivity improvement:
- Process Improvement

In Lean Manufacturing, standardized work is a means of establishing precise procedures to make products in the safest, easiest, and most effective way based on current technologies.

Standardized work is one of the principles of Lean Manufacturing. It requires three elements:

Takt time: Rate at which parts or products must be produced in order to meet customer demand.

Work Sequence: The steps operators need to perform within Takt time, in the order in which they must be completed.

Standard inventory (or in-process stock): Minimum quantity of parts and raw materials needed to run operations.

Benefits of standardized work

1. Reduces variability

By standardizing the most efficient way to perform processes, standardized work reduces variations in the output. Work becomes predictable: quality, costs, required inventory, and delivery times can be anticipated.

2. Helps your people

Shop floor operators are sometimes under the impression that their highly variable work cannot be standardized, or that implementing standards will make their work boring. Quite the opposite: enforcing standardized work increases efficiency, thus making more time for creative work. Standardized work also helps operators structure their work. It removes pressure on operators by reducing the stress of performing tasks improperly.

Finally, standardized work makes training much easier, since it documents the correct way to perform all processes. It ensures that new employees are given all the information needed to perform equally to other operators.

3. Improves continuous improvement

Kaizen, another Lean principle, is the concept of continuous improvement. Standardized work provides a basis for Kaizen. Indeed, it is only possible to evaluate improvements objectively when existing procedures are standardized and documented. As standards improve, the new standard for Kaizen becomes the basis for further improvements: improving standardized work is a never-ending process.

When operators perform tasks differently, it becomes more difficult to notice the 8 wastes of Lean Manufacturing in operations. In other words, it is easier to find opportunities for improvements when processes are consistent.

6 steps to apply for standardized work

1. Collect data on your current operations

The first step is to establish your work sequence and Takt time. Through IoT connected tools and cloud computing, modern manufacturers can collect data and measure Takt time automatically. Metrics such as cycle time and step time per operator are recorded consistently. Manufacturers gain real-time visibility into their operations, meaning they know exactly how tasks are currently executed.

2. Notice variations and issues

Often there are several ways to perform a task, but only one of these ways uses resources–materials, machines, and operators–in the most efficient way possible. Look at the data you have collected, and notice variations. Are there workers that perform the same tasks, but the output varies greatly? Are some operators taking longer than Takt time? Could some tasks be combined? Where is safety or quality issues occurring?

3. Find the most efficient way to run your operations

This is where you want to use Lean tools to optimize your work sequence and procedures. For example, you could use value stream mapping to identify non-value adding steps or poka-yoke to mistake-proof your processes. Your goal is to find methods that are practical, useful to everyone, and free of difficulty.

4. Document everything

There are many ways you can go about doing this. One of the simplest ways is in digital work instructions. Digital work instructions can be created with a manufacturing app. Media-rich and interactive; they guide operators through processes step by step.

Digital work instructions ensure that operators follow each and every step properly, according to the current best practice outlined by your standardized work. More importantly, digital work instructions can be modified in just a few clicks. Therefore, as your standardized work evolves, you can easily keep it documented and up to date.

5. Adapt your training programs

It is important that employees understand the new standard procedures and adhere to them. This might require re-training current workers. Furthermore, you want to make sure that your new operator training programs are based on your standardized work.

Similar to digital work instructions, digital training modules can be built in manufacturing apps and modified easily. Through videos, images, and other multimedia resources, new employees can self-guide their way through your most recent standardized procedures.

6. Continuously improve the standard

A common mistake is to think that after establishing standardized work, you are done. Instead, you should constantly strive to further improve the standard.

Once standardized work is implemented, it becomes a lot easier to identify abnormalities and issues. Perform root-cause analysis for every problem that occurs and create a new standard that solves the problem.

Standardized work is never perfect or final. It represents a current best practice that should be challenged on a daily basis with Kaizen.

Benefits of Standardized Work

The benefits of standardizing work processes are many and varied, and each organization will experience its own unique positive results. In general, standardized work delivers the following benefits:

Increased Efficiency

- Increases worker productivity
- Provides structure
- Saves time
- Makes waste more visible
- Cuts down on waste
- Establishes predictability
- Matches output with customer demand
- Makes issues easier to identify
- Allows workers to identify more areas for improvement
- Simplifies the employee onboarding process
- Flattens the learning curve
- Allows supervisors to focus on higher priorities

Improved Safety Measures

- Ensures best practices are followed
- Mitigates worker burnout
- Reduces workplace stress
- Establishes consistent safety protocols

Better Communication

- Makes workplace knowledge accessible to all
- Supports employee ownership and engagement
- Enables problem solving at all levels
- Gives workers tools to resolve issues
- Increases employee satisfaction and morale

Improved Financials

- Increases uptime and revenue

- Cuts down on operational costs
- Helps with budget planning
- Increases product quality and customer satisfaction

Who Benefits from Standardized Work?

By design, all parties related to an organization benefit from standardized work — from the CEO to the frontline leader to the consumer. More specifically:

Employees

Workers who follow standard work procedures experience more job satisfaction and a lower rate of burnout, since there is a far lower chance of making mistakes or experiencing miscommunication with co-workers or supervisors. Standardized work can also empower employees to identify areas for improvement, which can result in a sense of ownership and competency within their profession.

Supervisors

Whether they oversee a plant, department or frontline workers, supervisors who help to implement standardized work processes find that communication becomes easier and onboarding becomes less of a hassle. When workers know exactly what to do during their shift, supervisors can find more time to address higher-priority issues that will help the organization as a whole.

Executives

If operations within an organization become more streamlined, it can help cut down on waste, increase output and free up budgetary resources for allocation elsewhere. Improved productivity is good news for executives, as are better worker communication and improved safety measures.

Customers

When organizations have standards in place to address production, quality, customer service, order fulfilment and interdepartmental communication, customers are almost always guaranteed high-quality products, efficient and effective customer service and decreased wait times. When an organization can meet (or exceed) the customer's expectations, customer loyalty and satisfaction increases.

Standardized work can also be an answer to systemic issues organizations have struggled with in the past, including:

- Failure to sustain the results from past improvement strategies
- Problems keeping or training new employees
- Inability to guarantee or work within consistent timeframes
- Inability to keep up with demand OR overproduction when demand falls

How Does Standardized Work Drive Continuous Improvement?

Standardized work is not meant to be a rigid set of standard operating procedures. While work standards are established to simplify and define processes so that everyone across the workplace spectrum knows their responsibilities, the right standardized work training and coaching programs leave room for continuous improvement. It helps to think of standardized work procedures as the most current best practices, rather than rules carved in stone.

Standardized work as a methodology was developed by Mr. Isao Kato for the Toyota Motor Corporation as part of his decades-long commitment to improving production at the company's facilities, both in Japan and overseas. Kato based his standardization framework on the ancient philosophy of kaizen — literally, "small change." Kaizen emphasizes that large problems can be solved by addressing issues on a much smaller scale and making incremental changes over a period of time. Work standards act as anchor points for a thousand small issues which, if addressed using the kaizen principle, can result in positive change across an entire organization.

As Dr. Robert Maurer, author of The Spirit of Kaizen, says, "Standardization allows everyone to look for incremental ways to make improvements, even as you formalize the process." In a way, we can consider standardized work to be "structured creativity," as it leaves room for workers to identify areas for improvement and gives supervisors the tools to adapt strategies to suit multiple applications.

What Should Be Standardized?

Any element of work that occurs more than once and follows a regular process can be standardized.

Clear examples include machine or equipment operations, cleaning procedures, safety measures and packing protocols; less obvious examples can include customer service scripts, design processes and teaching (or training) frameworks. If supervisors or executives are wondering whether a process should be standardized, they can ask themselves or their employees what, if any, steps in a process could benefit from greater consistency. Chances are good that opportunities for standardization will be quickly identified.

When standardizing work, one needs to clearly define the content, sequence, timing and desired outcomes of the work. While it may be simple to imagine this process in a manufacturing context, for instance, let's use a slightly less intuitive example: a barber shop. But how can you standardize a haircut?

Every barber shop or hair salon has a process for booking appointments, shampooing and preparing clients' hair, cleansing tools and stations, assessing client needs, completing transactions and communicating aftercare instructions. While individual haircuts and client requests vary greatly, standardizing the basic procedures involved can promote efficiency, clear communication, cleanliness and overall customer satisfaction with the outcome.

Even with such variable content as a haircut, organizations can average the amount of time it takes to complete an entire process, and therefore can establish an effective daily schedule and even predict revenue for any given timeframe.

What Should Not Be Standardized?

Of course, any task that requires employees to use individual discretion or has no consistent process cannot be standardized. However, the framework around these variabilities can be standardized — even the process an artist uses to prepare can follow a set pattern of conceptualizing, sketching and gathering supplies. And every artist, whether they are painting a picture, writing a novel or playing jazz, employs basic patterns and skills they have learned and practiced even as they create their unique artistic contribution.

It takes time to identify how best to standardize procedures, so brand-new processes often pose a challenge. An excellent (and timely) example of this is the mass COVID-19 vaccination campaign that began in the U.S. in December 2020. Our country's health infrastructure had never experienced a campaign on such a massive scale, so a standard procedure needed to be established in order to vaccinate the most people in the shortest amount of time. By the time the general population was eligible for the vaccine — a mere four months later — most of the nation's 316 million-plus recipients experienced an orderly, efficient and quick procedure. Patient registration, check-in, shot administration, wait times and follow-up booking procedures were all standardized, so that people from San Diego to Boston shared very similar experiences. This was an unusual but crucial example of a rapid standardization that worked.

Every organization, big or small, has a standardized procedure for something. In order for this standard procedure to work, however, it needs to be used consistently. If a standard doesn't seem to be working for a particular application, chances are it has more to do with the implementation process, rather than the application's fitness for standardization. A certified trainer can help identify necessary changes, whether that means better training or slight adjustments to the standard.

How to Apply Standardized Work Methods

When an organization identifies the need for standardized work processes, it can be helpful to have the objective input of outside instructors. While these instructors may not be experts in your workers' specific fields, they will be able to spot excess waste (of time, energy, materials, etc.) and address areas that would benefit from standardization.

Standardized work principles can often be applied following this process:

1. Observe and collect data on your current operations and analyze your current output, internal interactions, costs and revenue, etc.
2. Take note of variations and issues in your processes or product quality.
3. Find the most efficient way to run your operations — this can be identified and developed with the help of a certified trainer.
4. Document everything along the way!
5. Improve your training and onboarding programs to lock in standards and break down knowledge silos.
6. Continue to improve the standards you develop.

During the instruction and implementation process, trainers will suggest using your organization's mission statement as a conceptual touchstone. A company's culture should be fully aligned with the development of its people, no matter their position, and should support continuous improvement.

An example of this is the Toyota Motor Corporation's motto: "Making things means making people." As the crucible for modern standardized work methods, Toyota upholds its mission by fostering a company-wide culture of continuous improvement. As long as workers and supervisors understand how standardization can support and further the organization's larger mission (and vice versa), they see the value of standardized work training.

Addressing Resistance to Change

Though most people within an organization can see the benefit of standardized work, it's not unusual for some members to express resistance. Some workers, especially those who have been doing their jobs for many years, don't see the value of standardization when they've been perfectly successful doing things their way. Supervisors, too, may take issue with being told by outside instructors how to manage their own departments.

This is where the Job Relations (JR) portion of a SW course comes into play. JR instruction — a component of TWI integration — teaches supervisors how to handle problems, enables positive interactions between co-workers and management and emphasizes teamwork as the bedrock for workplace success. Once they understand the outcomes of better communication and collaboration, many of those who are resistant to workplace change will agree that standardization will improve and not undermine their efficacy.

No matter the industry they're addressing, effective standardized work trainers know to keep an open mind in the classroom and will emphasize that their input is meant to help your organization's subject matter experts perform their jobs with fewer challenges. Rather than turning people into machines — or replacing them with automation — standardized work training aims to make workers' relationship to their work more meaningful, successful and satisfying.

Lean Project selection

The Lean Six Sigma methodology is implemented to significantly improve business processes. There is an in-depth focus on reducing and eventually eliminating waste and inefficiency. Eradicating problems and improving working conditions creates a more effective work environment and offers more precise responses towards meeting the needs of customers. But for this to happen, Selecting Successful Six Sigma Projects is the first step.

Understanding the criteria to assess the cost of a project to an organization in all capacities could be the difference between a profitable success and a draining loss. With 70% of organizations suffering project failure at least once over their last year of activity, reassessing the criteria for the selection process is necessary.

Introduction

The Lean Six Sigma framework is designed to phase out problems, reduce waste within the production process and inefficiency. It combines two of the strongest business methods to achieve maximum benefits for the organization; Lean principles (that focus on creating products and services using only what the production process requires) and Six Sigma (a method that focuses on increasing production efficiently and effectively).

In order to understand the value of selecting project that are Lean Six Sigma positive, the organization should introduce change in terms of;

- Tools and Techniques – Maximizing production through enhancing tools and production techniques that eradicate the waste during the process
- Process and Methodology – Equipping staff with production solving techniques and understanding the root of problems and tackling them from the ground up
- Mindset and Culture – Editing ground level processing capabilities to build a strong foundation that centers around bettering the organization as a whole

Parameters for Selecting Successful Six Sigma Projects

The project selection within an organisation is not only critical but difficult to execute to consistent success. While being able to identify a host of prospective opportunities is common, streamlining down to meaningful projects must include a well-defined framework. The benefits of undertaking a successful lean six sigma project revolves around three key steps;

Having a Project Selection Committee

The feasibility study must be conducted by Lean Six Sigma trained and certified employees. The team commonly referred to as "Six Sigma Champions", includes a manager, deployment champions, master black belts, and black belts. These employees bring an abundance of knowledge and adaptation abilities that allow them to carefully assess the value creation of executing projects.

Generating Project Ideas

Conducting a similar analysis to the SWOT (Strengths, Weaknesses, Opportunities, Threats) allows organizations to understand the practical undertaking of the prospective project. In order to generate viable Lean Six Sigma projects, businesses identify possible impacts on not only the organization but employees, customers, and other stakeholders.

Project Champions flow through a series of questions recognizing the impact on:

- Defect Reduction:
    - Was the waste created during the production process?
    - Were all produced items in line with the desired output specifications?
    - In the production of higher volumes, what has to be reworked to accommodate the output?
    - Is there any degree of variation in the output produced?
- Cycle Time Reduction:
    - Do any processes include multiple handovers between individuals to be completed?
    - Does the production process satisfy expectations?
    - Does the production process entail employees working beyond working hours?
    - Does the lag of mechanized elements significantly affect the production process?
- Resource Consumption Reduction:
    - Does the production process include materials of varying qualities?
    - How much labor is required to process parts of the production process?

Through this questioning process, a "Lean Six Sigma Project Tile" can be created. The tile includes a problem/need statement that defines the problem and the outcomes specific to the problem created. Vague statements are discouraged.

The current process impact is the second tile. It consists of quantifiable data and statistics that outline the current process and the results of the same. The third tile follows the Six Sigma Objective benefit. This tile explains the objective of the product with reference to utilizing six sigma. The positive outcomes of the organization are explained in detail.

Finally, the fourth tile covers deliverables and milestones. A timeline is established covering in detail the time in months and the expected phases of project completion. Key drivers to accomplish every phase are retailed in line with effective project completion.

Assess and Prioritize projects using a Project Selection Matrix

While conducting the internal project selection, all identified prospects are reviewed together to determine the most seamless integration possibility and possible benefits. Ongoing projects are simultaneously reassessed and, in the process, ranked according to a selection matrix. All projects are identified and numbered and ranked according to questions listed within project characteristics e.g., the likelihood of a project being completed within six months or whether a project would result in the development of quality improvement. When all projects are ranked, an overall pattern of success will reveal itself allowing for companies to decide their trajectory.

An assessment as to whether the project is also feasible to tackle utilizing DMAIC (Define, Measure, Analyze, Improve, and Control) is additionally conducted.

Lean Six Sigma has a martial-arts convention for naming most of its professionals. Each Lean Six Sigma professional is responsible for performing a particular set of duties within an organization. Each Lean Six Sigma role and the respective training required for that role have been outlined below:

1. **Champion**

The Champion, also commonly referred to as the Lean Six Sigma Leader, is an executive leader of the organization that is responsible for driving the Lean Six Sigma initiative. The Champion reports directly to the CEO of an organization.

A LSS Champion is accountable for the entire Lean Six Sigma deployment and supports the change by cultivating a Lean Six Sigma culture within the organization. This individual helps select projects, create a project charter, supervise projects on a weekly basis, and remove the barriers that might exist during project implementation.

Every organization can have only a single LSS Champion who is generally a senior-level executive of the company and has received high-level training regarding the technical aspects of Lean Six Sigma and is also equipped with the skills of leading an initiative.

1. **Master Black Belt**

A Master Black Belt (MBB), also known as the LSS Program Manager, is an experienced and successful Black Belt that has managed a number of Lean Six Sigma projects and is an expert in the methods and tools that are associated with Lean Six Sigma. A MBB reports to the LSS Champion of an organization.

The primary role of a Master Black Belt is to develop the Lean Six Sigma training program for an organization and coach project management teams. A MBB is also responsible for assisting in the selection of projects, supporting the efforts of the LSS Champion, and monitoring the Lean Six Sigma projects.

An organization can have a number of Master Black Belts for their Lean Six Sigma initiative but it must be ensured that a Master Black Belt is a full-time professional that is highly experienced and has successfully managed several projects as a Black Belt.

Preferably, a company with 10,000 employees should have up to 8 Master Black Belts by the fifth year of their Lean Six Sigma deployment.

1. **Black Belt**

A Black Belt (BB) is an individual that has advanced knowledge of Lean Six Sigma, particularly the methods and statistical tools, and possesses leadership qualities.

The role of a Black Belt is to coach, manage, and lead the project team for a Lean Six Sigma project. Each Black Belt in an organization is responsible for leading one (or more) DMAIC projects in an organization and ensuring that the right data is collected and analysed for the project(s).

A Black Belt is also responsible for identifying and communicating the barriers in a project and providing regular updates about the project to a Master Black Belt.

When choosing people for Black Belt training, ensure that you choose full-time professionals for your organization that have some team skills (which will be utilized in the training program). The selected individuals will then be required to attend classroom training for around four to five weeks where they will be taught about the methods, statistical tools, and technical concepts of Lean Six Sigma.

Once a Black Belt has received their training, they should be required to manage a 'test' DMAIC project to assess their skills. As with Master Black Belts, a company with 10,000 employees should have up to 50 Black Belts by the fifth year of their Lean Six Sigma deployment.

1. **Green Belt**

A Green Belt is a part-time professional for an organization that has some expertise about Lean Six Sigma (sufficient for leading a small LSS project).

The exact role of a Green Belt depends on the requirements of an organization but generally, a Green Belt is responsible for assisting a Black Belt with one of their projects and for providing just-in-time training to others. However, if there is a need, a Green Belt might also be required to start and manage their own project under the direct supervision of a Master Black Belt.

For selecting individuals for Green Belt, make sure that you choose a part-time professional for your organization that is willing to learn about the Lean Six Sigma process. The training program for Green Belts will require the chosen individuals to attend classroom training for a maximum of two weeks in which they will be taught about the methods and basic statistical tools of Lean Six Sigma.

Ideally, a company of 10,000 people should have up to 200 Green Belts by the fifth year of their Lean Six Sigma deployment.

1. **Team Member**

Any professional in an organization that has general awareness or basic knowledge of Lean Six Sigma and can contribute to a particular project (through expertise and experience) is considered to be a LSS Team Member.

It is important to mention here that a team member does not need to have any sort of formal Lean Six Sigma training. Though the role of such individuals is not well-defined in Lean Six Sigma, a team member can be anyone that provides expertise, provides data and resources, and helps identify opportunities for improvement for a project.

The team members are generally more involved with an organization's work and business processes and therefore, they can help in selecting the right DMAIC projects for the Lean Six Sigma initiative since they can see exactly where the improvements are needed in a business' workflow.

One common mistake that is made by most organizations is that they only choose technical specialists (such as statisticians, engineers, and quality professionals) as team members. For a successful and efficient implementation of Lean Six Sigma, it is important to incorporate the management (such as senior managers and process owners) as team members, as well.

1. **Process Owner**

A Process Owner is a professional that is responsible for a particular process within a business and is accountable for achieving the desired performance for that process.

Since each DMAIC project is aimed at solving a problem and improving the efficiency of a particular process, the process owner (for that specific process) must always be part of the Lean Six Sigma team. There is no need for formally training the Process Owner regarding Lean Six Sigma, though a short briefing will be beneficial for the sake of the project.

The role of a Process Owner is defined by the Champion or Master Black Belt depending on the requirements of the project. However, the responsibilities of a Process Owner are to assist the Black Belt in the decision-making, data collection, and process improvement phase of a project.

1. **Project Sponsor**

The Project Sponsor is a business executive that is responsible for providing the budget, resources, and strategic directions for the project team so that they can move further with the project implementation. This individual is also responsible for removing the barriers (particularly financial barriers) that could slow down the project's process.

Towards the end of a project, the Project Sponsor is responsible for celebrating the success, communicating it to all departments, and recognizing (and awarding) the key players of the project.

Again, each DMAIC project will have only one Project Sponsor that will act as a facilitator and a supervising body for the project.

We have already discussed how you need to go about convincing and informing the executives to sponsor a Lean Six Sigma project. Every Project Sponsor should be well informed about the Lean Six Sigma process and should be involved in the communication process for Lean Six Sigma.

Forming A Lean Six Sigma Team

Now that you know exactly what roles each individual has in a Lean Six Sigma organization, let us take a look at everything that you need to know about forming a Lean Six Sigma team for a project.

1. **How Many People Should Be There?**

You should appoint no more than six people in a Lean Six Sigma team. Each team member should be familiar with the involved process and should contribute towards the implementation of the Lean Six Sigma solution.

The reason that the team should not have more than six members is because a large team can be ineffective since the responsibilities are diluted and it is more difficult to reach a consensus.

If you feel as though a project cannot be completed by six people then the project is too large and complex and should be split into two or more smaller projects.

1. **Who Should Be A Part Of The Team?**

There must always be a Black Belt (team leader) and a Process Owner associated with each project. Additionally, a Green Belt should be included in the team, if necessary.

The remaining members should be Lean Six Sigma team members who are available at least 25% of the time for working on the team and should be familiar with the process that has to be improved.

While a Project Sponsor is generally considered to be associated with a Lean Six Sigma project, they are not counted as a core team member since they are not directly responsible for implementing the solution or taking any action towards the process improvement.

1. **Who Should Form The Team?**

The best approach towards forming a team is for a Black Belt to consult with the Master Black Belt, Head Of Divisions (the managers to whom the potential team members report to), Project Sponsor, and the Champion (if possible).

The Black Belt first directly consults with the Master Black Belt and/or Champion to discuss the potential team members.

After this, the Black Belt gets approval from the team members' respective Head Of Division to include them on the team.

Once this is done, the barriers to the project are identified and reported to the Project Sponsor and/or Champion who resolve the issues before the project can be implemented.

Any additional training that might be required by the team members can be directly delivered by the Black Belt or Green Belt before the work on the project begins.

Introduction to Lean Planning

Planning is defining the steps and the resources required to achieve a desired outcome.

The lean project itself is a plan to create net value for the customer and the other stakeholders. Lean planning is not a separate phase of the project cycle, but takes place in each phase, as part of the PDCA cycles. In terms of the flow of value, the project plan is a design of the project value stream.

The primary purpose of lean project planning is to enable the achievement of project objectives by informing decision making and defining the means and actions. Planning reduces uncertainty, establishes trust and facilitates a reliable flow of value. Plans are means of transparency, collaboration, alignment, direction and coordination.

Planning is often seen as the dividing line between traditional project management and Agile. But there is nothing wrong with considering project management as plan-driven. Regarding planning, the difference between the "traditional plan-driven" and the "agile-driven" project management isn't the presence or absence of a plan. The major difference is that traditional planning is more "predictive" than adaptive, while Lean-Agile planning is more adaptive rather than predictive, and it's generally more intense. "Predictive" planning tries to plan the unknowable, which is both wasteful in itself and causes waste. Adaptive planning plans how to make unknowable knowable and thus effectively increases predictability.

Each lean project plan is a combination of a plan to execute and a plan to experiment and validate. A plan to execute can work for what's known, while a plan to experiment and validate should aim at acquiring knowledge and reducing risk of what's unknown. The right proportion between the two depends on the specific circumstances, but the mental setting of the team should be that each project is a hypothesis that they need to prove empirically.

Lean acknowledges that results are not completely knowable in advance, and planning must be adaptive. The value of a plan is perishable and may change because of:

- New knowledge gained about customer value, stakeholders' expectations, requirements, deliverables, creation process, technologies, project team, risks and assumptions
- Empirical evidence about team's productivity
- Stakeholder feedback on deliverables increments
- Changes in project environment
- Revised estimates and forecast of project's net benefit
- Any discoveries and new information that affect the project

PDCA Cycle and Planning

In the Initiation-Planning-Execution-Closing cycle of traditional project management, the important component of learning and improvement is missing. Thus, planning itself is also not subject to systematic improvement.

In lean project management, we should view planning as part of the Plan-Do-Check-Act (PDCA) cycle through which we realize the project objectives.

It may seem that PDCA is a single and unified cycle, but in fact, we should consider it as composed of individual cycles for each of its phases. The planning PDCA cycle promotes continuous improvement and includes:

- **Plan**: planning how to carry out the planning process
- **Do**: performing planning
- **Check**: checking the quality of planning
- **Act/Adjust**: learning and improvement of the four planning processes (plan planning, do planning, check planning, adjust planning)

This is an example of continuous improvement of planning :

- Determine the percentage of completed activities from the total number of planned activities over a given period (Percent Plan Complete – PPC). PPC measures plan reliability.
- Identify causes for noncompletion.
- Act – remove the causes to improve planning and aim to increase PPC.

Here is how we can improve plan value and reliability:

- Perform continuous estimating and planning
- Assess the plan's value and reliability on a cadence
- Actively remove constraints to the workflow to improve plan reliability
- Learn and adapt to improve plan value and reliability

Planning Constraints

The project plan must ensure that we achieve the best outcome within the existing constraints. Constraints are set by external circumstances, third parties, the customer or other stakeholders. Let's look at how constraints affect planning and how to set constraints which are under the direct control of the customer and the project team.

There can be many constraints in a project, but the common ones are time, cost, scope and, to some extent, quality. For some types of projects, regulations and location are also very important.

Besides the legal factors, probably the only constraint that we should consider fixed by default is the minimum required profitability of the project. Without achieving it, the project makes little sense. Conditions of Satisfaction follow next, but they are negotiable.

Traditional project management assumes that, through proper upfront planning, we can precisely define the project scope and we may not need to change it. In turn, the fixed scope makes it possible to assess and fix time and cost within tight tolerances. It turns out, however, that projects can rarely be completed within a fixed scope, time and cost. Instead of over-constraining, we need flexibility in one or more of these variables.

Fixing scope

We can define project scope as the configuration of project deliverables with their features, functions and relationships. As the primary consideration for the scope is benefit and cost, it should be quite normal that it varies to improve the outcome.

Typically, we can achieve project objectives through an unlimited number of alternative scope configurations. Fixing one of all possible configurations means that we consider it to be complete and the best one at the outset of the project. This is equivalent to accepting that a hypothesis needs no proof or deciding with incomplete information. Therefore, we don't recommend fixing the scope. Instead, we might consider certain range limits of scope, based on experience with similar projects.

The progressive detailing, narrowing, prioritizing and improving of the scope begins with the choice of project approach, goes through different stages as, for example, a choice of design option, and goes on until the very end of the project.

Fixing scope often results in including items that are not absolutely necessary. A better solution might be to leave open the possibility to prioritize scope items within the other project constraints. The Minimum Viable Project (and the Minimum Viable Scope respectively) is also a good approach to prevent fixing a scope that is too large.

Fixing time

From a practical point of view, we will always have some kind of time limit. Projects don't go on indefinitely.

Apart from regulatory requirements, the primary rationale for limiting time should be the cost of time.

Another aim for fixing time along with cost might be to ensure that we complete high-value work by a fixed date when we correctly prioritize scope items.

A third reason for fixing time might be to foster innovation, when we set a stretch goal for cycle time improvement.

Fixing costs

We must always consider the total life cycle costs of the project and the expected benefit-cost ratio. From a customer's perspective, operation, maintenance and business costs are expected to be financed from the revenue, and a constraint usually applies to investment costs. The limits depend on the customer's available funds (there is always some limitation) and the amount they are prepared to invest (the target cost).

When the customer sets a target cost, the project team should aim to optimize the configuration of scope, time, quality and recurrent costs to maximize the return. Therefore, constraining the costs is a valid approach, unless the target cost doesn't accomplish a minimum viable project.

Planning Items

Planning items provide guidance for executing the project. The project scope is translated into planning items such as milestones, stages, iterations, user stories, features and tasks, and dependencies between them. In turn, the planning items drive resource requirements and cost and time estimates that provide feedback for refining the scope (see more about estimating).

Milestones

Milestones are the backbone of the overall project schedule. These are events that mark significant stages in the project's progress and facilitate flow – key decisions, deliverables, handoffs, and coordination and integration points that release subsequent major stages of work.

Milestones aggregate individual activities and are more reliable than them, as they pool variability from independent sources.

Stages

Stages are common building blocks of the non-iterative evolutionary life cycle. Stage planning is the first (macro) level of detailing the plan in terms of the local (stage level) milestones, tasks, dependencies, sequence, and priorities. The next level of increasing detail could be the regular look-ahead planning that also emphasizes making tasks ready for execution and removing constraints.

Iterations

These are the key components of the iterative life cycle. Iteration is a time-boxed PDCA work cycle aimed at creating an increment of project assets that can be absorbed into the customer's value stream. If absorbed, we expect the increment to improve the capability of the value stream which would generate incremental value.

Lean Manufacturing: The Practical Approach to Productivity

A lean manufacturing initiative focuses on cost reduction and increases in turnover by systematically and continuously eliminating non-value-added activities. In today's competitive market, lean is turning out to be "the solution" to manufacturing industries across the spectrum for survival and success.

Lean manufacturing helps organizations to achieve targeted productivity and more by introduction of easy-to-apply and maintainable techniques and tools. Its focus on waste reduction and elimination enables it to be engrained into organization culture and turns every process into a profit centre.

Thousands of companies worldwide have achieved tremendous productivity and return on investments by implementing lean practices and techniques. India has witnessed many success stories in its automotive, process and other industries. See also: Overall Equipment Effectiveness OEE

In a nutshell, lean manufacturing is all about driving toward achieving profitability and productivity through continuous improvement and resource waste elimination. It is an organizational culture as well as specific practices with clear goals.

The road map to lean manufacturing and its benefits were discussed at a recent seminar hosted by Bangalore, India-based Axcend Automation & Software, a manufacturing IT solutions company. Senior-level delegates from various multinational and national companies pitched in with their perspective on lean during this half-day event.

In today's competitive world, while large-scale companies have taken the first steps to implement lean in their organizations, small and medium establishments (SMEs) also need to follow the lean thinking and implement the same to achieve their set goals.

S.D. Janakiram, lean advisor for public-sector enterprise HAL, set the theme for the event, mentioning that the company has embraced "Sampoorna Paravarthan" (complete change) to implement lean. He reiterated the fact that implementing lean is a collective achievement, where every single member's dedication and perseverance makes it a success.

Lean is about achievement orientation and execution excellence. There is a need for shift in thinking to "a zero tolerance for waste". Persistence for improvement, learning by doing, attitudinal changes and teamwork, along with emphasis to bring value quickly and remove waste continuously, form the essence of lean.

Mr. Janakiram concluded by saying that the mantra for success has four Ps – Purpose & Process as intellectual issues connected to the brain and Pride & Passion gives the heart dimension.

While lean is to be definitely achieved, how can it be done? What are the tools required? Providing answers to this was Gary Flum, the general manager for advanced manufacturing systems at QAD. Taking into account QAD's longstanding relationship with manufacturing industry, Flum gave the enterprise IT perspective of achieving lean. He presented the lean solution available from QAD that could be implemented even in SMEs.

He started off with the evolution of the automotive industry, mentioning that the dichotomy of successful manufacturing is cost and innovation. Plotting a curve of value associated with phases of innovation, Flum mentioned that the challenge is to keep the value derived through innovation growing; continuous innovation allows you to stay ahead of the cycle of common acceptance.

Flum went on to present how overhead costs in an enterprise were directly reduced due to implementation of lean. He concluded by mentioning that lean manufacturing focuses on the value stream and by showing the advantages of implementing lean and just-in-time in manufacturing.

Lean is a generic process management philosophy derived mostly from the Toyota Production System (TPS), hence it was definitely relevant for Toyota to speak on this. T.R. Parasuraman, general manager of Toyota Kirloskar Auto Parts (TKAP) spoke about best practices of manufacturing and its benefits.

Elimination of three Ms – muri, mura and Muda – is important and forms the basis of TPS. Touching upon the 5-S methods, Parasuraman reiterated the need to passionately practice it to achieve global standards. If quality is lost, everything is lost. Emphasis on quality is supreme and any failure needs to be analyzed in depth to get the root cause.

“Rejection is a treasure” said Parasuraman, reiterating the Toyota way of handling quality problems. He concluded by offering his Ten Commandments of Quality.

Overall, the delegates were enabled with the seminar’s objective for inducing and practicing lean thinking. Today, it is relevant that any organization that has set its goal to be a global player or a regional leader has to incorporate changes to be productive and competitive. Lean manufacturing shows the way to that goal.

Lean process improvement identifies which working processes are valuable and which are inefficient.

This strategy aims to **streamline workflows, minimize wastage, manage inventories, mitigate redundancies, improve quality,** and nurture value-added working processes, which ultimately, passes on value to the customer. Generally, lean process improvement seeks to make incremental changes to existing protocols. These augmentations are made at strategic moments, adopting a phased approach to optimizing working processes. As such, **the goal of every lean process improvement initiative is to ensure all tasks and workflows are efficient and effective** throughout the entire supply chain. Therefore, lean process improvement enhances the customer’s perceptions of value and overall satisfaction.

Moreover, **the more value the customer places on a product, the more they are willing to pay.** Thus, lean process improvement has a direct relationship to revenue. Furthermore, efficient processes and reduced waste improve overall operational productivity. This, in turn, **enables businesses to increase their profit margins and overall return on investment.** As such, lean process improvement is a critical activity when it comes to reaching broader corporate goals. In this article, **we discuss the key steps of lean process improvement** and how professionals should implement these measures within their organization.\

1. Analyse the process that needs to improve

The first and most important step of lean process improvement is **studying and understanding the current processes in place and how they function.** A helpful approach is an AS-IS mapping model, which graphs a given process and its phases. This generates a comprehensive picture of what could be causing delays or bottlenecks and where improvements can be made. Further to this, **it is important to conduct interviews with the employees involved in the process in question.** After all, there is no one who will know better than them where improvements can be made.

2. Identify improvements

After the analysis stage, **the project team needs to model the proposed process improvements.** Create another diagram and share ideas; the new model should consider the purpose of the activity; who is most qualified to implement it; where the quality and compliance issues are, and why are they occurring. **Remember to build this model from the ground up,** considering why the task is necessary, where it should be carried out, and what the existing problems are.

3. Implementation

After process modelling, the team needs to **plan how to implement their suggested changes.** Effectively actioning proposals and promoting organizational buy-in is an essential component of the success of the project. Once the new ideas are in place, the project managers can assess whether or not the improvements will succeed long-term.

4. Execution and monitoring

Improvement is only possible with careful monitoring and management. Once a project is properly assessed and measured, the project team can refine the execution. Managing execution is another critical step in lean process improvement, as the **execution sequences will generate new indicators that drive further developments.** However, there is of course always the chance that this new process will uncover different bottlenecks. As such, the importance of the monitoring stage is further emphasized, as **the identification of new issues leads to enhanced process optimization and further productivity gains.**

5. Value-added activity

Assessing value is an essential component of the project monitoring process: **does each activity within the process add value to the company's service or product?** If the answer is yes, then the team must seek to continually improve this activity, to ensure maximum value is transferred to the consumer. However, **if an activity is shown to be of little value, the project team should eliminate it** from the process with immediate effect.

6. Mitigate the risk of faults

Some processes may include risky activity. Operational streamlining is, in essence, risk-averse. Therefore, the project team should seek to eliminate or simplify the activity. For example, **there may be a technological solution that mitigates the risk of processual faults.** However, organizations should not necessarily assume that automation is always the answer; sometimes, human resources will hold the solution to the desired improvement.

7. Standardization

In some instances, a process will repeat throughout the value chain. These occurrences should be **properly documented and stored in an accessible process library.** This will promote the democratization of information across the enterprise, ensuring that when departments design new processes, they have detailed information about how other areas operate. As such, **these tools will promote the standardization of processes and more efficient management.** Thanks to recyclable components, departments can work together to create integrated processes.

8. Compliance

Process improvement is not a finite endeavour. **It is essential that the concept of lean process improvement permeate company culture,** ensuring that employees apply these principles on an ongoing basis. However, most industries have standardized measurements, procedures, certifications, and other monitoring metrics. Subsequently, these measurements are overseen by government departments or industry standards bodies. Obviously, **process improvement projects cannot contravene these rules.**

9. Enhancing customer experience

It is essential that the advantages of lean process improvement are passed on to the customer. **Without enhanced customer experience, all the efficiencies and improvements are rendered almost meaningless.** Therefore, customer experience needs to be carefully assessed; this final stage is what marketers refer to as "the moment of truth", where the impact of process improvement reveals itself.

Questions

1. What is standardized and explain the elements of standardized work?
2. Describe the process of applying standard work?
3. How will standard work benefit the organization?
4. What work should be standardized and what should not explain?
5. Explain the process of applying standard work?
6. How to select a six-sigma project?
7. Explain different roles in six sigma project committee?

References

1. Prado-Prado, J. C., García-Arca, J., Fernández-González, A. J., & Mosteiro-Añón, M. (2020). Increasing competitiveness through the implementation of lean management in healthcare. *International Journal of Environmental Research and Public Health, 17*(14), 4981.
2. da Costa Nogueira, D. M., Sousa, P. S., & Moreira, M. R. (2018). The relationship between leadership style and the success of Lean management implementation. *Leadership & Organization Development Journal.*
3. Cadden, T., Millar, K., Treacy, R., & Humphreys, P. (2020). The mediating influence of organisational cultural practices in successful lean management implementation. *International Journal of Production Economics, 229*, 107744.
4. Asnan, R., Nordin, N., & Othman, S. N. (2015). Managing change on lean implementation in service sector. *Procedia-Social and Behavioral Sciences, 211*, 313-319.
5. Emiliani, M. L. (2008). Standardized work for executive leadership. *Leadership & Organization Development Journal.*
6. Fin, J. C., Vidor, G., Cecconello, I., & de Campos Machado, V. (2017). Improvement based on standardized work: an implementation case study. *Brazilian Journal of Operations & Production Management, 14*(3),

388-395.

7. Pereira, A., Abreu, M. F., Silva, D., Alves, A. C., Oliveira, J. A., Lopes, I., & Figueiredo, M. C. (2016). Reconfigurable standardized work in a lean company–a case study. *Procedia Cirp*, *52*, 239-244.
8. Misiurek, B. (2016). *Standardized work with TWI: Eliminating human errors in production and service processes*. CRC Press.
9. Halim, N. H. A., Jaffar, A., Yusof, N., Jaafar, R., Adnan, A. N., Salleh, N. A. M., & Azira, N. N. (2015). Standardized work in TPS production line. *Jurnal Teknologi*, *76*(6).
10. Martin, T. D., & Bell, J. T. (2017). *New Horizons in Standardized Work: techniques for manufacturing and business process improvement*. CRC Press.
11. Ray, S., & Das, P. (2010). Six Sigma project selection methodology. *International Journal of Lean Six Sigma*.
12. Kumar, M., Antony, J., & Cho, B. R. (2009). Project selection and its impact on the successful deployment of Six Sigma. *Business Process Management Journal*.
13. Sharma, S., & Chetiya, A. R. (2010). Six Sigma project selection: an analysis of responsible factors. *International Journal of Lean Six Sigma*.

Abrevations

TPM -Total productive Maintenance

OEE- Overall Equipment Effectiveness

VSM- Value stream mapping

KPI- Key performance indicators

TPS- Toyota production system

SKU- Stock keeping units

ELS- Economic lot size

COGS- Cost of goods sold

WIP- Work in progress

JIT- Just in time

JR- Job relations

SW- Standard work

TWI- Training with industry

SWOT- Strength, weakness, opportunities, and threats

DMJAC- Define, measure, analyse, improve and control

CEO- Chief executive officer

LSS- Lean six sigma

MBB- Master black belt

BB- Black belt

PDCA- Plan, do, check, act.

PPC- Percent plan complete

www.ingramcontent.com/pod-product-compliance
Ingram Content Group UK Ltd.
Pitfield, Milton Keynes, MK11 3LW, UK
UKHW021915190726
13853UKWH00002B/691

9 798886 848786